EMPLOYER ACCOUNTING FOR PENSION COSTS AND OTHER POST-RETIREMENT BENEFITS

BY HAROLD DANKNER
MICHAEL P. GLINSKY
JOHN H. GRADY
MURRAY B. HIRSCH
RICHARD M. STEINBERG

A research study and report prepared for the
FINANCIAL EXECUTIVES RESEARCH FOUNDATION

Employer Accounting for
Pension Costs and Other
Post-Retirement Benefits

Financial Executives Research Foundation
633 Third Avenue, New York, New York 10017

International Standard Book Number—0-910586-42-X
Library of Congress Catalog Card Number—81-68568
Printed in the United States of America
M 2003

As the research arm of Financial Executives Institute, the basic objective of the Research Foundation is to sponsor fundamental research and publish authoritative material in the field of business management with particular emphasis on the principles and practices of financial management and its evolving role in the management of business.

Publication of a research study should not be interpreted as constituting endorsement by the Board as a whole, or by individual Trustees.

FOREWORD

The assets of private pension funds are now well in excess of $300 billion and are growing at a rapid pace. Effectively operating and funding pension plans has become a major responsibility for financial and other executives. Moreover, both active and retired employees are showing an increasing interest in the financial status of their company's pension plan.

Congress has also shown a great interest in regulating the funding and general operation of private pension plans. The Employee Retirement Income Security Act of 1974 (ERISA) established minimum standards for fiduciary conduct for trustees, administrators, and others dealing with retirement plans. In addition, minimum standards were established concerning participation, vesting, funding, and reporting and disclosure.

The future of private, as well as public, pension plans has become an important current social and political concern. A number of groups, including the President's Commission on Pension Policy, have studied in a broad, long-term context such important issues such as coverage, equity, retirement income security, financing, tax incentives, and inflation.

In light of the importance of pension plans, it is essential that we have accounting that provides information about employer's pension costs and pension obligations which is relevant, reliable, and understandable. In this regard, the Financial Accounting Standards Board (FASB) has already issued an interim Statement No. 36 on disclosure of pension information, and is working on a comprehensive re-examination of employer accounting for pension costs and other post-employment benefits. According to the Chairman of the FASB, the overall pension project is one of the most important undertaken since the Board was established in 1973.

These developments are cause for deep concern for executives of the one-half million organizations with private pension plans. How should executives react to legislative proposals for further pension controls? How should they respond to the various proposals that have been put forth by the FASB?

To obtain the answers to these questions, we turned to Coopers & Lybrand. They are acknowledged to be leaders in matters relating to pension costs, and they probably have in-house many of the best available actuaries. We wish to thank them for their excellent work.

We believe the information in this volume will be of great value to financial executives as they wrestle with the difficult problems of accounting for the costs of pensions and other post-retirement benefits. We heartily recommend it and urge you to use it to good advantage in helping to deal with the accounting and other problems surrounding the management of pension plans.

Charles R. Allen, President
Financial Executives ResearchFoundation

ABOUT THE AUTHORS

Harold Dankner, CPA —Mr. Dankner is a Partner and Director of Research and Technical Services for the Actuarial, Benefits and Compensation Consulting practice of Coopers & Lybrand. He consults on a wide variety of problems involving the design of retirement plans, financial reporting of pension costs and other benefits, taxation of benefits, ERISA reporting and disclosure, executive compensation, acquisitions, ESOPs, and retirement and financial planning. Additionally, Mr. Dankner is responsible for the development of technical policies, client communications, and liaison with regulatory agencies which include IRS, DOL, and PBGC. Active in the corporate employee benefits field for 13 years, he has served as a tax law specialist with the national office of the Internal Revenue Service and authored numerous articles on employee benefit plans.

Michael P. Glinsky, CPA — Mr. Glinsky is a Partner at Coopers & Lybrand in the New York City Office. He is a General Practice Partner and has special expertise in the following industries: communications, cable television, and electric utilities. He is also an expert in the area of operational auditing and computer auditing. Mr. Glinsky is a member of the American Institute of Certified Public Accountants and has been active in their Regulated Industry Committee. As a member of the New York State Society of Certified Public Accountants, he recently has been active in the Entertainment and Sports Accounting Committee.

John H. Grady, FSA — Mr. Grady is a Partner in Coopers & Lybrand's Actuarial, Benefits and Compensation Consulting Division. He has participated in several major actuarial consulting engagements for governmental units and presently serves as the consultant and enrolled actuary for a number of large corporate pension plan clients. Mr. Grady is a Fellow of the Society of Actuaries, and a Fellow of the Canadian Institute of Actuaries.

Murray B. Hirsch, CPA — Mr. Hirsch is the National Director of Professional Education for Coopers & Lybrand. Until April 1, 1981, he was the Regional Partner-in-Charge of the Actuarial, Benefits and Compensation Consulting offices of Coopers & Lybrand in Atlanta, Boston, Chicago, Detroit, and New York. Prior to joining Coopers & Lybrand as a General Practice Partner in 1975, Mr. Hirsch was President and Chief Executive Officer of a major manufacturer and retailer of men's clothing. Prior to that date, he was a Partner in another large CPA firm with which he had been associated for 18 years.

Richard M. Steinberg, CPA — Mr. Steinberg is a Partner in the Auditing Directorate in Coopers & Lybrand's National Office. His responsibilities include formulating audit-related policies and providing guidance to the practice on emerging issues, as well as leading the Directorate's computer audit activities. When ERISA was enacted, he developed a broad range of policy and related technical material, and served as a consultant to the practice on pension accounting, auditing and regulatory requirements. Mr. Steinberg is a member of the AICPA Committee on Pensions and ERISA and the AICPA Task Force on Pension Plans and Pension Costs, and is co-author of the book, *Pensions—An Accounting and Management Guide,* and a number of articles and monographs on pension matters.

ACKNOWLEDGMENTS

The basic research, survey, and modeling analyses required the combined efforts of a number of people. In this connection, we wish to express our special appreciation to the following members of Coopers & Lybrand's professional staff for their considerable assistance:

Marguerite Heilman
Patricia Peterman
Bruce Redmon

We also wish to thank the Project Advisory Committee and Benjamin Makela, Research Director of the Financial Executives Research Foundation, for their valuable advice concerning the study and report. In addition, we express our gratitude to the many corporate executives and others who were involved with the preparation or use of financial statements and actuarial information for their participation in the interviews and mail survey.

Table of Contents

ONE

EXECUTIVE SUMMARY

Pension plans have become an increasingly significant aspect of the U.S. economy. Over 30 million people are covered by approximately a half million private pension benefit plans and millions of additional employees are participants in governmental plans. Assets of private pension plans totalled more than $321 billion in 1979; assets of federal, state, and local government pension systems amounted to another $200 billion.

The question of whether present accounting practice meaningfully presents the financial effect of an employer's pension plan responsibilities has received significant attention in the financial press during the past few years. Of particular concern is the magnitude of unfunded pension obligations. Many corporate executives and experts in the employee benefits field, however, believe that the unfunded pension obligations issue is exaggerated. They contend that these unfunded amounts should not be of great concern as long as the plan sponsor's financial condition is sound; the key factor is whether the plan sponsor can continue to make required pension plan contributions. The Financial Accounting Standards Board is studying this issue and other related complex questions in its comprehensive re-examination of employer accounting for pension costs. As an interim measure, the FASB issued Statement No. 36, "Disclosure of Pension Information," in July 1980. The scope and timing of the FASB's overall project is:

1

- A discussion memorandum covering only the basic issues was published in the first quarter of 1981.

- A document that contains the FASB's tentative conclusions on those basic issues and discusses additional issues is scheduled to be issued in early 1982.

- An exposure draft and later a final statement of financial reporting standards is to be issued in 1983.

With the objective of providing substantial authoritative data on the issues, the Financial Executives Research Foundation (the research arm of the Financial Executives Institute) retained Coopers & Lybrand to conduct an extensive study on accounting for pension costs and other post-retirement benefits. To obtain the needed data, Coopers & Lybrand organized the study into three phases:

Phase I—Research to identify the issues and accounting alternatives.

Phase II—Interviews and a mail survey to obtain the views of plan sponsors (issuers of financial statements), users of financial statements, consulting actuaries, independent public accountants, and other interested parties on the issues and alternatives identified in Phase I.

Phase III—Computer modeling to present quantitative analyses of alternative actuarial and accounting methods.

BASIC RESEARCH—IDENTIFICATION OF THE ISSUES

To identify and analyze the issues affecting accounting for pension costs and other post-retirement benefits, we examined current literature by experts in the fields of employee benefits, accounting, and finance. Furthermore, we utilized the extensive experience and knowledge of our Firm's actuarial and accounting personnel.

Important background information is presented in Chapters Two and Three. In Chapter Two, "A Perspective: The Nature and Growth of Pension and Other Post-Retirement Benefits," we focus on important characteristics of pension plans, foreign plans, termination indemnities, and post-retirement health and death benefits.

Chapter Three discusses basic actuarial principles that are central to accounting for the costs of defined benefit plans. We discuss actuarial assumptions—the factors (interest, mortality, etc.) considered by an actuary when estimating the total benefits ultimately to be paid by a plan and the present value of those benefits. An explanation of how the various actuarial methods allocate the estimated present value of future benefits as a cost to past, current, and future years follows. Chapter Four discusses the accounting principles that currently apply to pension costs and other post-retirement benefits.

A detailed analysis of the major issues and alternatives is presented in Chapter Five. These issues include:

- Should an obligation for pension costs be recognized as an accounting liability on the sponsoring company's balance sheet?
- How should the obligation be measured?
- How should actuarial assumptions be selected in determining the obligation?
- Should an obligation be recorded or disclosed net of plan assets?
- How should plan assets be valued?
- How should the annual expense provision be determined?
- What should be the relationship between expense and the obligation?
- Which disclosures are appropriate?
- Should the costs for post-retirement health and death benefits be accrued over the employees' working lives?

Alternative answers to these and other questions are discussed in detail. For example, we consider a number of alternatives for measuring a pension obligation, including unfunded vested benefits and the present value of accumulated benefits.

MAIL SURVEY AND INTERVIEW FINDINGS

A basic objective of the survey and interviews was to obtain the views of plan sponsors, consulting actuaries, independent public accountants, financial analysts, and others who are involved with the preparation or use of financial statements and actuarial information.

Using our research data, we developed a single, comprehensive questionnaire for use in the mail survey and interviews. After testing the questionnaire, 2,511 copies were mailed to selected respondents and 37 respondents were contacted to participate in the interviews. We received 398 usable responses from the mail survey and interviewed 30 respondents, which gave us a total of 428 responses, representing an overall response rate of 17%. This exhibit shows the makeup of the total group of respondents by type.

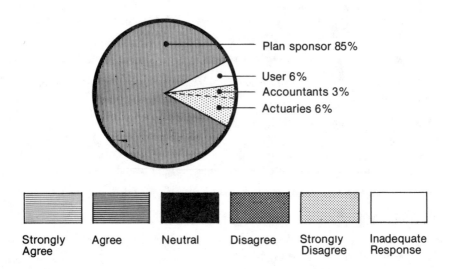

Strongly Agree	Agree	Neutral	Disagree	Strongly Disagree	Inadequate Response

A summary of our findings and observations on certain key issues is presented here. Chapter Six describes our methodology and findings in greater detail. The questionnaire, with tabulated results for the mail survey, is an appendix to Chapter Six.

SUMMARY OF FINDINGS AND OBSERVATIONS ON CERTAIN KEY ISSUES

- **Use of Pension Cost Data is Limited.** Respondents who are financial analysts, creditors, and other users of financial statements reported that pension cost data appearing in sponsoring employers' financial statements are not likely to substantially alter or reverse credit or investment conclusions. Interview respondents generally indicated that the information is not very useful. A number of interview respondents also indicated that, for some credit analyses, pension costs are imputed as part of the fixed costs of a company's operations. For example, all or a portion of unfunded prior service costs may be treated as debt. This is generally the case when there is concern about a company's ability to meet its obligations.

- *Majority of Respondents Oppose Liability Recognition.*   A majority of the respondents (61%) disagreed with the statement that some measure of a pension obligation should be recorded as an accounting liability; 29% indicated that a liability should be recorded.

  Categorizing respondents by "user," "plan sponsor," and "other" does not result in a significant variance in the response pattern. However, when the "other respondent" group is broken down into its two major components (i.e., consulting actuaries and independent public accountants) the response pattern changes considerably. The response attributable to the consulting actuaries is clearly negative (69% disagreed), while the independent public accountants' response is strongly positive (73% agreed).

  Of those respondents who indicated that some measure of a liability should be recorded, most favored using either vested benefits or accumulated benefits as the measure of the obligation. Only 8% favored PBGC guaranteed benefits. It is also noted that the largest percentage of respondents (50%) agreed that if one single measure of the obligation is required to be disclosed, it should be vested benefits.

- *Most Respondents Are Opposed to Mandating an Actuarial Cost Method or Assumptions to Determine Expense.*   Most respondents (over 73%) disagreed with an alternative that would require all sponsors to determine expense, using the same actuarial method. Only 15% of the respondents agreed with this alternative. Many interview respondents observed that a choice of an actuarial cost method should be allowed based on the characteristics of the sponsor's plan and the sponsor's financial forecast. The point was made that every plan and sponsor is unique. They noted that companies are allowed to have a choice among acceptable methods in other accounting areas such as depreciation and inventory valuations.

  The response to two options that would limit the choice in actuarial assumptions (one option would prescribe specific quantitative amounts while the second option would prescribe specific types of actuarial assumptions) was also decidedly negative—76% disagreed with specifying quantitative amounts (12% agreed); 55% disagreed with specifying specific types (31% agreed).

- *Respondents Indicated that Pension Expense is Most Important.* The respondents clearly identified pension expense as the most important aspect of assessing a sponsoring employer's pension costs. The next most important items are: "Some measure of an obligation and the value of plan assets," "The amount actually funded for the period," and "The actuarial cost method and assumptions used for expense purposes."

- *Disclosure Considerations.* In response to several items of disclosure required by FASB Statement No. 36 or the preceding exposure draft, most respondents (70%) agreed with disclosure of the actuarial present value of vested benefits. As to the other items, 68% agreed with disclosure of the fair market value of the plan's assets available for benefits; 57% agreed with disclosure of a description of significant actuarial assumptions and asset valuation methods; 55% agreed with disclosure of the assumed rate of return; and 52% agreed with disclosure of the actuarial present value of accumulated benefits.

  A number of interview respondents expressed concern that if too much information is disclosed, confusion could result. For example, undue alarm could result from focusing on incorrect relationships, such as pension expense as a percentage of total revenues. Many respondents also were concerned that too much importance might be placed on pension cost information relative to other financial statement data.

- *More Guidance Needed on Plant Closings.* A majority (52%) of the respondents disagreed with the statement that an obligation for unfunded vested benefits relating to employees of the closed plant arising as a result of the plant closing should be charged immediately to income. We note that a relatively large number of respondents (14%) did not know or did not give an answer. Furthermore, many interview respondents observed that more guidance is needed in accounting for work force reductions in general, whether or not a plant closing occurs. Others voiced concern about the appropriate measure of an accounting liability in the event of a plant closing.

- *Multiemployer Plans—Concern About Availability of Data and Impact of New Multiemployer Plan Law.* We asked whether employer accounting for multiemployer defined benefit plans should be subject to the same accounting rules as single-employer defined benefit plans. More than one-third of the respondents did not know enough about the issue to respond, were neutral, or simply did not respond. We note that 70% of the plan sponsors responding to our survey do not make contributions to a multiemployer plan. Of those respondents who make contributions to multiemployer plans, 30% indicated that employer accounting for multiemployer plans should be the same as for single employer plans while 47% disagreed and 23% either did not know, were neutral, or did not respond.

A number of interview respondents indicated a concern about the availability of good data and the unknown impact of the Multiemployer Pension Plan Amendments Act of 1980. Since the new law is extremely complicated and required data is just now being produced, we share this concern.

- *Treatment of Foreign Plans.*   Generally, more respondents agreed (rather than disagreed) that employer accounting for costs related to foreign defined benefit plans should be subject to the same accounting rules as domestic plans. However, when examining the response from companies who maintain foreign plans, the number of respondents who disagreed increases considerably. In this regard, many interview respondents expressed concern about the availability of information, the cost to produce required information, and the significance of the information.

- *Post-Retirement Health and Death Benefits—Current Practice.*   Nearly all of the respondents account for the expense on a "pay-as-you-go" basis (96% for health benefits and 82% for death benefits). We note that most respondents reported expense of less than 1% of payroll for post-retirement health and death benefits. In addition, the greatest number of respondents reported pension expense of 5% to 10% of payroll. However, pension costs are generally expensed over the working lives of employees—making any comparison with other post-retirement costs unrealistic.

- *Disclosure.*   The survey response indicates that a greater percentage of respondents favor disclosing the existence of other post-retirement benefits than the other possibilities (47% agreed, 33% disagreed). However, we note that many respondents (approximately 25%) did not answer or were neutral on the question of disclosure. In addition, the interview respondents appeared to be less knowledgeable about post-retirement benefits (when compared to pension plans) and offered fewer comments. Moreover, respondents observed that:

  - • the costs are not likely to be material,
  - • methodology needs to be developed to estimate and allocate costs, and
  - • if disclosures are to be required, work needs to be done to obtain more data about existing plans.

- *Expense.*   More than half the respondents indicated that a single method for accounting for the expense associated with other post-retirement benefits should not be required (52% agreed, 23% disagreed). Of the methods offered as options only (a) pay-as-you-go received an overall positive response (41% agreed, 34% disagreed). However, many respondents (about 28%) did not answer or were neutral on the question of expense. This again indicates a lack of formulated opinions concerning the treatment of other post-retirement benefits.

MODELING ANALYSES

The basic objective of our modeling analyses was to examine the quantitative impact of various factors on pension obligation and expense, including:

- Actuarial cost methods to determine expense;
- Alternative obligation measures;
- Nature and experience of the plan membership;
- Plan provisions; and
- Actuarial assumptions.

We performed our analyses by creating a model consisting of:

- Three model pension plans with common benefit formulas based on final pay, career average pay, and a unit benefit (fixed amount) per year of service,
- Three model plan populations exhibiting different characteristics and experience over a 50-year period, and
- A set of actuarial assumptions for valuing obligation and expense for the model plans.

In addition, we examined the impact of alternative accounting treatments (e.g., recording an unfunded obligation as a liability) on a company's financial statements.

A summary of key findings and observations follows. We note that the findings and observations apply only to our illustrative model. Different results might be obtained under other facts and circumstances. Chapter Seven describes our methodology, findings, and observations in detail.

SUMMARY OF KEY FINDINGS AND OBSERVATIONS

Obligation Measures: The obligation measure selected has a significant effect on the size of the obligation. Our analyses indicate that the obligations under the various measures were generally within a range of 80% to 150% of the present value of accumulated benefits. Under certain obligation measures, however, the obligation exceeded 200% of the present value of accumulated benefits.

Actuarial Cost Methods: The pattern of pension expense can vary materially among acceptable actuarial cost methods. The cost methods producing the lowest amount of pension expense in the initial years produced the highest amount of expense in later years of the projection period. The variation in pension expense was generally 50% or less in each year.

Plan Membership: Changes in the characteristics of the plan membership (e.g., growth or decline in number of active participants may have a substantial impact on the pattern of pension expense). For example, we found that for a plan with a declining membership, the pattern of pension expense will remain stable as a percent of compensation under certain actuarial cost methods but will rise dramatically under other methods.

Plan Benefit Formula and Pension Obligation: A plan's benefit formula may have a significant effect on the size of the obligation. We found that differences in the size of the obligation may result even when different benefit formulas provide identical benefits. The pension obligation under the model final average pay plan generally exceeded the obligation under the career average pay and unit benefit plans by 15% to 25%.

Plan Benefit Formula and Pattern of Expense: Although the three model pension plans provide equivalent benefits, we found different patterns of expense under certain actuarial cost methods. When we calculated expense as normal cost plus 30-year amortization of past service cost and prior service cost resulting from plan amendments, the career average and unit benefit plans had lower expense initially and higher expense later in the projection period when compared with the final pay plan.

Actuarial Assumptions and Pension Obligation: Interest and salary assumptions generally have the greatest impact on the size of the pension obligation. For the model final pay plan, an increase in the interest assumption from 7% to 8% produced a decrease in obligation of 10% to 14%, under all the alternative measures. An increase in the salary scale assumption from 6% to 7% produced an increase in the size of the obligation under the alternative measures between 0% (the present value of accumulated benefits) and 8%. A simultaneous increase of 1% in both the interest (7% to 8%) and salary (6% to 7%) assumptions reduced the obligation under certain measures by approximately 8%.

Actuarial Assumptions and Pension Expense: The impact of a change in the salary and interest assumptions on expense depends not only on the actuarial cost method, but also the degree to which the prior service cost has been funded. In general, the impact of a change in these assumptions is greater as the degree of prior service cost funding increases. Depending on the actuarial cost method and degree of funding of prior service cost, a 1% increase in the interest assumption from 7% to 8% decreased expense by 15% to 27%, a 1% increase in the salary scale assumption from 6% to 7% increased expense by 9% to 25%, and a simultaneous 1% increase in both the interest (7% to 8%) and salary (6% to 7%) assumptions decreased expense by 8% to 15%.

Alternative Accounting Treatments: Our analyses considered three alternative accounting treatments with model company financial statements:

- Continue current accounting treatment under APB Opinion No. 8 (no pension obligation recorded, pension expense determined by an actuarial cost method).

- Implement a new accounting standard which records the unfunded pension obligation with an immediate charge to income. Pension expense is determined each year based on the change in pension obligation.

- Implement a new accounting standard which records the unfunded obligation with an offsetting deferred charge to be amortized over a period of years. Annual pension expense is generally determined based on the change in pension obligation, however, changes in obligation due to certain occurrences (e.g., plan amendments, actuarial gains or losses) are not charged immediately to income but are offset by deferred charges to be amortized over future years.

Our analyses found that recording the unfunded obligation with an immediate charge to income produces a significant decrease (almost 45% under one obligation measure) in the sponsor's net income in the year this accounting treatment is implemented. In subsequent years, this treatment produces lower pension expense and higher net income than either current accounting treatment or a standard which records the unfunded obligation with an offsetting amortizable deferred charge.

The analyses also show that in other typical situations (e.g., implementation of a new plan, amendment of an existing plan, or a change in actuarial assumptions), determining pension expense based on the change in pension obligation can result in sharp increases or decreases in pension expense from year to year. Both current accounting treatment and the alternative treatment which offsets certain changes in obligation by amortizable deferred charges results in a leveling of expense which avoids these wide fluctuations.

As a result of the study, the Coopers & Lybrand research team developed certain observations and opinions on accounting for pension costs and other post-retirement benefits. These observations are presented in Chapter Eight and should be construed as solely the views of the Coopers & Lybrand research team and not those of the Financial Executives Research Foundation Project Advisory Committee or anyone else connected with the study.

TWO

A PERSPECTIVE: THE NATURE AND GROWTH OF PENSION AND OTHER POST-RETIREMENT BENEFITS

The provision of pension benefits is firmly established as a normal and necessary cost of doing business in the United States. Over the past 40 years, pension funds have substantially grown in number and size.

Before examining the accounting issues (Chapter Five) it is important to focus on certain highlights in the historical development of pension plans and other post-retirement benefit programs. The chapter has a brief review of the:

- Historical development and growth of pension plans.
- Types of domestic pension plans.
- Basic features of a defined benefit plan.
- Important laws affecting pension plans.
- Future legislation and important studies.
- Foreign plans and termination indemnities.
- Post-retirement benefits other than pensions.

HISTORICAL DEVELOPMENT AND GROWTH OF PENSION PLANS

Origin and General Philosophies of Private Pension Plans

No single, social, or economic philosophy fully explains the growth of pension plans. Instead, there are many significant factors and events that have encouraged employers to establish plans for their employees.

In the late nineteenth century, American industrial concerns started providing pensions to retirees, generally in recognition of past loyalty. These pensions were granted on an informal, almost casual, basis. In effect, the pension amounts and the recipients were determined at the discretion of the employer.

The informal approach to granting pensions carried into the twentieth century. In the early 1900's formal pension plans were largely confined to government employees and the employees of railroads and utilities. However, even in cases where there was a formal plan, benefits were generally defined by the courts as an inchoate gift to which the employee had no legal right.[1] Most pension plans were designed to impose no legal liability on the employer.[2] Usually, formal plans specifically stated that no employee rights were being created under the plan and that the employer reserved the right to deny, reduce, or terminate benefits. A few plans promised to continue benefit payments to retired employees but made no commitment to active employees.[3]

Groups seeking to encourage the growth of private pension plans argued that employers had a moral obligation to provide pensions to superannuated employees. It was argued that "no employer had the right to engage men in any occupation that exhausts the individual's industrial life in 10, 20, or 40 years, and then leave the remnant floating on society at large as a derelict at sea."[4] Critics of this *human depreciation philosophy*, pointed out that aging is not a result of employment but of physiological processes.[5] However, the minimum vesting standards later established by ERISA (1974) support the concept that an employer who uses the services of an employee for an extended period has an obligation to make some contribution toward the individual's retirement.

Another philosophy considered a pension *deferred wages* for services performed during an employee's working life. The major fault with this theory was that electing a pension in lieu of wages would be valid only if the pension was ultimately paid (i.e., all pensions would have to be fully vested).

Still another philosophy held that businesses used pension programs to meet the social problem of old-age economic dependency. A pension grant came to imply that payments would continue to the employee throughout retirement, and that similar consideration would be given to current employees. In many instances, past service pension improvements for current employees and pension increases for retirees are granted to encourage current employees to provide future service. This has been evident in the collective bargaining process in many industries such as the steel industry.

Thus, pension plans gradually became a part of employment policy, and businesses began to realize the desirability of making advance provisions for pensions they expected to pay active employees when they retire.

Factors Influencing the Growth of Pension Plans

The significant growth in pension programs in the United States has occurred since the 1940's as a result of several factors:

- *Wage Stabilization.* The wage stabilization program imposed during World War II prohibited employers from paying higher wages. The War Labor Board attempted to relieve the pressure for increased wages by permitting companies to establish fringe benefit plans, thus stimulating the growth of pension plans.

- *Union Demands.* Labor's drive for pension benefits was substantially aided by the *Inland Steel Company* case, which established the principle that employers were legally obligated to bargain over the terms of pension plans in labor negotiations. A union grievance filed with the National

Labor Relations Board against the Inland Steel Company stemmed from the company's refusal to negotiate its policy on normal retirement age. In 1948, the National Labor Relations Board ruled that pension plans were subject to mandatory collective bargaining in that they constitute both "wages" and "other conditions of employment" under the National Labor Relations Act of 1947.[6] The Court of Appeals for the Seventh Circuit affirmed the view of the National Labor Relations Board.[7]

- *Tax Incentives.*   For many years, tax advantages to both the sponsoring employer and the employees covered by qualified retirement plans have helped stimulate plan growth. These advantages include:

  - • Current deductibility of contributions by the employer, within certain limitations.
  - • Exemption of the plan's related trust from income tax.
  - • Deferment of income to the participating employees until the benefits are distributed or otherwise made available to them.
  - • Favorable income tax treatment for certain lump sum distributions from plans.
  - • Favorable estate and gift tax treatment to participating employees and their beneficiaries.

- *Increased Productivity.*   Businesses learned that senior personnel were less reluctant to retire when they were assured of some degree of financial security after leaving the company. Formal pension plans were established to meet those employees' needs, thereby giving the company the opportunity to hire and promote younger, more productive personnel.

- *Employer Competition.*   Employees eventually came to expect a pension plan to be part of their compensation package. Since businesses without pension programs were often at a competitive disadvantage, many companies established pension plans to help attract and retain personnel.

Current Status of Pension Plans

A recent government survey of pension plan coverage estimates that in 1979 more than 30 million people—about 50% of all private wage and salary workers—were covered by private pension, profit-sharing, or other retirement plans.[8] There are about a half million pension, profit-sharing, and stock bonus plans in the United States. In 1979, these plans paid approximately $20 billion in benefits to about 14 million beneficiaries.[9]

The assets of pension plans have also increased dramatically in recent years, as shown by these figures for 1978:

- Assets of private pension plans totalled more than $321 billion.[10]

- Federal retirement systems have accumulated assets of $57.7 billion, invested in government securities.

- State and local government pension systems had approximately $142.6 billion[11] in assets, mainly invested in private securities.

In summary, through their pension funds, employees of American business, together with public employees and teachers, own about 35% of business' outstanding equity capital.[12]

TYPES OF DOMESTIC PENSION PLANS

An employer can establish a pension plan unilaterally (a conventional or voluntary plan) or through collective bargaining between employer(s) and employees (a negotiated plan). A plan established as the result of bargaining between a labor union and one or more companies is sometimes referred to as a pattern plan, and terms of the plan are adopted (perhaps with variations) by companies in the same or allied industries.

Pension plans are established either by a single employer or a group of affiliated employers (single-employer plans) or by several employers in one or more industries. Some single-employer plans are unilaterally established; others are collectively bargained. Multiemployer plans are usually established under collective bargaining agreements and are jointly managed by representatives of labor and management.

A qualified pension plan is a plan that conforms with Internal Revenue Code requirements. As discussed earlier, qualified plans have certain tax advantages (e.g., exemption of the pension trust from income tax). Nearly all formal private pension plans are qualified.

A qualified plan can be either a *defined contribution plan* or a *defined benefit plan.* Under a *defined contribution plan,* each participant has a separate account, and benefits are based solely on the balance in that account. Actuarial calculations are not required to determine the employer's annual contribution. The employer's contribution is generally expressed as a percentage of compensation (as a flat dollar amount or by a formula which may be indefinite) calling for the company's board of directors to determine the contribution by written resolution, as in the case of many profit-sharing and stock bonus plans. Earnings and expenses of the trust are allocated to each participant's account on an annual basis. Examples of defined contribution plans include money purchase pension plans, profit-sharing plans, stock bonus or employee stock ownership plans, and "target" or "assumed" benefit plans.

A *defined benefit plan* provides stated retirement benefits based on a fixed formula. Separate accounts are not maintained for each participant. There is no specific or definite contribution formula and actuarial calculations are required to determine the amount of the employer's annual contribution.

BASIC FEATURES OF A DEFINED BENEFIT PLAN

Some of the basic features of a defined benefit plan are:

- *Eligibility.*   Under some plans, employees may become eligible immediately when hired, regardless of age or prior service. Many plans, however, have adopted the minimum participation standards of ERISA—attainment of age 25 and completion of one year of service.

- *Vesting.* Employees have a vested interest if they are entitled to a present or future benefit without continuing in the employer's service. Under graded vesting, the initial vested right may be to receive in the future a stated percentage of a pension benefit based on years of credited service. The percentage may thereafter increase with additional years of service or of age until the right to receive the entire benefit has vested.

- *Normal Retirement Benefits.*   A variety of methods are used for determining retirement benefits. Benefits may be the same for all participants with specified periods of service (e.g., $300 per month for participants with 20 or more years of service); this is known as a flat benefit. A variation is a benefit based on years of service (e.g., $10 per month for each year of service). In many instances, however, benefits are based on each year's compensation (sometimes with fixed minimum and maximum amounts) and the total benefit is said to be on a career average compensation basis. Alternatively, the compensation base may be determined by average earnings during a specified period, such as the final three or five years of service (final average pay or final pay plan).

Many plans coordinate (i.e., integrate) their benefits with Social Security retirement benefits. This may be provided for in the benefit formula by applying a lower percentage to the part of earnings covered by Social Security or by reducing the benefit amount by a portion of the Social Security benefit.

- *Form and Duration of Retirement Benefits.* Retirement benefits may be paid in a lump sum, over the employee's remaining lifetime (a life or straight-life annuity), or over a longer period (period certain and life or joint and survivor annuity).

IMPORTANT LAWS AFFECTING PENSION PLANS

A number of important laws have influenced the development, design, and maintenance of pension plans. Some highlights of key legislation are very briefly discussed here.

Internal Revenue Code Requirements

Internal Revenue Code requirements are critically important to employers because of the tax advantages of having a qualified pension plan. Generally, in order to be qualified, a plan must be written, communicated to the employees, funded, and intended to be a permanent program. There are extensive procedural and substantive requirements for qualified plans, and the applicable qualification rules are intended to prevent discrimination in favor of highly compensated employees.

The Welfare and Pension Plan Disclosure Act of 1958

The primary objective of this law was to prevent mismanagement of plan assets by mandating certain disclosures to the Department of Labor. Title I of ERISA repealed and replaced this Act.

The Employee Retirement Income Security Act of 1974 (ERISA)

ERISA was primarily designed to:

- Establish minimum standards of fiduciary conduct for trustees, administrators, and others dealing with retirement plans.

- Provide for enforcement of these fiduciary standards through civil and criminal sanctions.

- Require adequate reporting and disclosure of administrative and financial affairs for plans.

- Improve the equitable character and soundness of private pension plans by requiring them to:

  - • Vest the accrued benefits of employees having significant periods of service with an employer.
  - • Meet minimum standards of funding.
  - • Guarantee the adequacy of plan assets against the risk of plan termination.[13]

ERISA provisions relevant to accounting for pension costs generally include:

- Required annual reports;

- Minimum funding requirements; and

- Termination insurance coverage for defined benefit plans.

These provisions (briefly described below) do not apply to church and governmental plans.

- ***Required Annual Reports.***   Plan participants have the right to obtain a copy of the full annual report, in addition to automatically receiving a summary of the annual report that does not include the plan's financial statements.

- ***Minimum Funding Requirements.***   These provisions apply to defined benefit plans:

  - • Sponsors must make annual minimum contributions equal to normal cost plus amortization over 30 years of unfunded liabilities for all plan benefits.

- • Plans may generally amortize unfunded liabilities existing as of the beginning of the 1976 plan year over 40 years.
- • Experience gains and losses are to be amortized over no more than 15 years for single-employer plans.

The IRS may waive the funding requirements on a year-by-year basis (up to 5 waivers in a 15-year period) if hardship can be demonstrated. Failure to meet the minimum funding requirements can result in a 5% excise tax being levied on the employer. An additional 100% excise tax may be imposed for failure to correct funding deficiencies after receiving IRS notification.

An employer may contribute an amount in excess of the minimum funding requirements and still be entitled to a tax deduction for the entire contribution. Provisions independent of the minimum funding requirements are used to determine whether pension contributions are tax-deductible.[14]

- *Termination Insurance Coverage for Defined Benefit Plans.* About one-fifth of all pension plans, covering approximately 60% of all plan participants, are defined benefit plans. These plans are usually insured by the Pension Benefit Guaranty Corporation (PBGC). ERISA authorized the establishment of the PBGC for the principal purpose of guaranteeing the timely and uninterrupted payment of limited amounts of vested pension benefits to participants and their beneficiaries when a defined benefit plan is terminated. In the case of a single-employer plan, the PBGC currently guarantees payment of all nonforfeitable basic benefits (other than benefits that become fully vested due to the plan's termination) in the form of a monthly benefit subject to prescribed limitations. The overall guaranteed monthly benefit, which is a life annuity commencing at age 65, may not exceed the actuarial equivalent of the lesser of:

  - • 100% of the average monthly wages during the individual's highest-paid 5 years of participation in the plan, or
  - • $750.

The $750-per-month maximum benefit is subject to adjustment based on changes in the level of the compensation base for Social Security purposes and for 1981 the maximum benefit is $1,281.[15]

In general, for new plans (and increases in benefits under plan amendments), the maximum limitation is to be phased-in generally for all individuals at the rate of 20% per year so that the benefit (or the increase) will be fully covered after it has been in effect for 5 years.[16]

An employer is liable to the PBGC for benefit payments made by the PBGC upon termination of a single-employer plan. The liability is an amount equal to the lesser of:

• The excess of the current value of the plan's guaranteed benefits on the date of termination, over the current value of the plan's assets, or

• 30% of the employer's net worth, computed without regard to this plan termination liability.

The Multiemployer Pension Plan Amendments Act of 1980

Under the Multiemployer Pension Plan Amendments Act of 1980, a company withdrawing from a multiemployer pension plan is exposed to unlimited liability instead of the 30%-of-net-worth limit. Further, the liability is to the plan, not the PBGC. The new law also increases the responsibilities of both multiemployer plans and contributing employers since plan insolvency, not plan termination, is now generally the insurable event, and funding requirements will continue to apply to terminated plans.

This highly complex law also changed the definition of a multiemployer plan and provided new rules pertaining to guaranteed benefits and employer withdrawal liability.

FUTURE LEGISLATION AND IMPORTANT STUDIES

The future of pension programs has become an important social and political concern. Policy decisions on pension issues—coverage, equity, retirement income security, financing, tax incentives, inflation, and retirement age—are now being considered in a broad, long-term economic context. Among the groups studying these issues are:

• The President's Commission on Pension Policy, with a mandate to examine public and private pensions.

- An independent National Commission on Social Security appointed by Congress and the President.

- Congressional committees and task forces.

Based on these concerns, it is generally expected that more pension-related laws will be passed to address coverage and other issues.

FOREIGN PLANS AND TERMINATION INDEMNITIES

Foreign Plans

In many foreign countries, private pension plans generally supplement government old age, survivor, and disability benefits. Foreign pension plans, which vary in terms and funding, are strongly influenced by local laws and employment practices. For instance, pension plans in the British private sector are almost always funded. This is due to a tradition of strict actuarial supervision, the fact that most plans are financed in part through employee contributions and the example set by some of the important public plans. The available funding methods are annuity contracts offered by life insurance companies and pension funds directly invested, with tax treatment the same for both. Generally, smaller plans are insured, larger ones self-invested.

A tax-deductible book reserve system became popular for many foreign plans following World War II when liquid capital available for employers was scarce. Today, additions to reserves are generally determined according to specified actuarial principles. Companies make provisions in their accounts without actually setting money aside. Book reserves are used in varying degrees to finance benefits in Austria, Belgium, West Germany, Italy, Luxembourg, Spain, and Sweden. In the Netherlands, a tax-deductible book reserve can be established for a past service pension liability in addition to traditional segregated funding.

Employees are given legally binding promises, but because neither they nor pension beneficiaries are generally preferential creditors under the book reserve system there may be no ultimate security. This factor was of growing concern in Germany until compulsory insolvency insurance was introduced in 1974. A small premium must now be paid to a special institution, which guarantees the pension rights of both retired employees and active members vested in accordance with the legal provisions.

Termination Indemnities

Termination indemnities—generally mandatory payments by employers as compensation to terminating employees—are an important feature of social legislation in more than 50 countries. Payments may be required by law, negotiated labor agreement, or employment contracts. Circumstances determining the right to payment and the amount vary from country to country. An indemnity may be payable for long service, an interrupted career, or a combination of the two. Although the most common indemnity is for involuntary termination without cause, indemnities are also payable in many countries for voluntary termination, retirement, death, disability, and sometimes, involuntary termination with cause.

In countries where notice is required before termination, the party initiating the termination must usually "give notice" with length of notice often determined by employee rank and years of service. Normally, an employer will indemnify the employee for the notice period rather than delay departure, particularly where plant closings are involved.

In many instances, obligations under termination indemnities are substantial. Benefits are usually based on years of service and final monthly wage rate. In some countries, benefits vary depending on whether they relate to voluntary or involuntary termination, termination with or without cause, or termination due to death, disability, or retirement. In many countries, the indemnity payable as a result of an involuntary termination is twice that due for a voluntary termination.

Only a few countries have advance funding and accounting requirements for termination indemnities. In Venezuela, for example, the law states that "book reserves" must be maintained by employers for each employee, and interest must be credited on accumulated obligations at specified rates. Brazilian employers must actually deposit funds equal to 8.33% of wages into segregated accounts. In Italy, specific book reserve requirements are based on current salary and cumulative years of service. In most countries, though, there are no legal funding or accounting requirements for termination indemnities. Partly for that reason, U.S.-based management of some multinational companies may not fully appreciate the potential size of the obligations until they become payable.

POST-RETIREMENT BENEFITS OTHER THAN PENSIONS

In addition to providing pension benefits, many companies extend other benefits to employees after retirement. The most popular post-retirement benefits, health and death benefits, are briefly discussed here.

Health Benefits

Since its inception in 1965, Medicare has ensured that retirees age 65 and older will have basic health care insurance. Medicare coverage is divided into two parts:

- Part A provides basic hospital benefits and is financed through compulsory hospital insurance taxes on employers and employees.

- Part B is a voluntary program designed to supplement Part A by covering the cost of physician services and a number of additional medical expenses. This supplemental coverage is financed through premiums paid by enrollees and through matching federal government contributions. The current premium for Part B is $9.60 per month.

While statistical data on current practices is generally scarce, a 1979 survey revealed that 39% of the surveyed companies offered retirees health insurance to supplement Medicare.[17] In addition, 14% of the surveyed companies paid at least part of the retiree's premium for Medicare Part B, and 30% of these companies paid the entire premium. Data from another survey of approximately 450 companies indicated that 88% of the companies provide post-retirement medical benefits to supplement Medicare.[18]

The monthly Medicare Part B premium had increased from $3.00 in 1966 to $9.60 in 1981. As a result of this steady increase, some companies pay only a fixed dollar amount towards the Part B premium, and the retiree pays the difference. Frequently, companies that pay the retiree's Medicare Part B premium also pay the premium for the retiree's spouse.

In addition to assisting a retiree in financing Medicare Part B coverage, there are generally three basic approaches a company can take to supplement a retiree's Medicare benefits:

- **Flat Dollar Payment.** The simplest method is to provide a flat dollar amount for each day of hospitalization. Thus, a hospitalized retiree might receive $40 per day, regardless of the nature of the illness or the total medical costs.

- **Add-On Plan.** The add-on or Medicare supplement plan generally provides a fixed benefit designed to pay expenses that are not covered by Medicare. The specific items to be covered and the percentage to be paid are determined by the company in designing its plan. For example, a Medicare supplement might provide reimbursement for a percentage of the retiree's Medicare B deductible and co-insurance. Thus, the supplemental plan could be designed to cover a percentage of uncovered hospital expenses, surgeon's fees, drugs, and medicines. Under an add-on or Medicare supplement plan, a company can tailor coverage specifically to its retiree population.

- **Offset Program.** Under an offset or Medicare carve-out program, an employer continues covering retirees under the same health plan provided for active employees, and benefit levels for both groups are identical. In operation, the offset plan provides the benefits that are not provided by Medicare. Typically, the plan establishes a level of benefits and states that costs reimbursed by Medicare will not be reimbursed by the plan. As a result, benefits under the offset plan are formally integrated with Medicare benefits.

Financing Post-Retirement Health Benefits

Companies typically finance post-retirement health benefits on an out-of-pocket basis. This would, of course, occur when a company assists a retiree in financing Medicare Part B coverage. In instances where a company provides additional benefits, they are often financed in the same manner as the basic health benefits for active employees.

Death Benefits

Among the significant changes brought about by ERISA was the requirement that qualified retirement plans provide survivor protection for a retiree's spouse. In addition to any death benefits provided under a company pension plan, a number of companies continue retiree life insurance protection. A survey conducted by the Bureau of National Affairs in 1979 found that 53% of the responding companies extend life insurance coverage to retirees. Of these companies, 16% maintain the level of coverage provided during active employment and 84% reduce retirees' coverage levels. In another survey by Hewitt Associates of salaried employee benefits, 86% of the surveyed companies provide some post-retirement life insurance.

Death benefits provided to retirees can take many forms. Some companies provide only a nominal flat dollar benefit, such as $5,000. This amount may be sufficient to cover funeral expenses and is therefore commonly referred to as burial insurance.

A death benefit may be based on a retiree's salary, position, or insurance level prior to retirement, and a company might provide a higher level of death benefits to former officers than it does to other employees. On the other hand, the same amount of post-retirement death benefits may be provided to all retirees. Also, a sliding scale of benefits could be provided, with reductions made in the benefit level for each year after retirement.

Death benefits may be paid in a lump sum or in installments. One method of providing death benefits to a retiree's beneficiaries is the survivor income plan. This plan is designed to continue income to beneficiaries for life or for a specified period. Survivor income is usually a percentage of the retiree's final pre-retirement compensation.

Financing Post-Retirement Death Benefits

A company can finance post-retirement death benefits in several ways. Some companies prefund benefits during the active life of the employee. Other companies pay these benefits out-of-pocket, terminally fund the benefit, or buy yearly renewable term insurance to provide the benefits.

The cost of yearly renewable term insurance for individuals over 65 is extremely high. For example, a recent survey of typical life insurance costs found that the cost for an individual aged 65 could be $31.75 per $1,000 of coverage, with the cost increasing about $3.00 for each year after age 65.[19] Consequently, companies using this method normally reduce retiree coverage to a nominal amount after age 65. Nominal coverage is also fairly common when death benefits are paid out-of-pocket. Typically, companies that pay a $5,000 death benefit to a retiree's spouse will do so out-of-pocket. (Since the tax laws exclude from income the first $5,000 paid by a company in the event of the death of an employee or former employee, this amount has become a common survivor benefit.)

Permanent life insurance, either on an individual or group basis, is one way to provide paid-up insurance coverage at retirement. The advantage of this method is that companies may avoid the increased cost of insurance coverage at higher ages by paying level premiums over the employee's working lifetime. There are, however, certain disadvantages to this method of funding. Permanent insurance requires an investment of company funds which could be used to meet other business objectives. Further, the rate of return the company receives on its investment in insurance may be less than the return on its other investments.

Group term life insurance is the most popular method of providing life insurance protection to employees. Some companies use a combination of group term and group permanent to meet the objectives of covering both active and retired employees. This combined arrangement has been called Section 79 permanent insurance, because it incorporates the concept of group term insurance, as well as providing a cash value policy which can be used to furnish post-retirement benefits.

Retired Lives Reserves

The retired lives reserve concept was developed specifically to deal with post-retirement death benefits. Basically, the reserve is established in conjunction with a company's regular group term program for active employees. Part of the company's annual contribution for group term life insurance protection is used to create a reserve that will be available to provide group term life insurance protection to retirees.

A retired lives reserve may be held by an insurance company, pursuant to a rider added to the company's group term insurance contract, or it may be held by an employees' trust. Typically, the reserve is established without allocation to individual employees. While retired lives reserves may be structured as an allocated fund, covered employees have no right to receive their allocation in cash.

Contributions to the reserve are actuarially determined and made on a level annual basis. Principal and income are used to pay premiums on group or individual policies that provide current coverage. The reserve also generates the premium needed to purchase paid-up insurance for retirees thereby providing coverage until death. Individual and group annuity contracts, as well as cash value life insurance policies, may also be used to accumulate the reserve fund and meet premium obligations.

An alternative to the insurance reserve, is a reserve established under a tax-exempt employees' trust. Section 501(c) (9) of the Internal Revenue Code provides an exemption from income tax to a voluntary employees' beneficiary association providing for the payment of life, sickness, accident, or other benefits to the members of the association.

NOTES

1. *McNeven v. Solvey Process Co.*, 32 App. Div. 610, 53 N.Y. Supp. 98 (4th Dep't 1898), *aff'd without opinion,* 167 N.Y. 530, 60 N.E. 1115 (1901).
2. Benjamin Aaron, *Legal Status of Employee Benefit Rights under Private Pension Plans* (Homewood, IL: Richard D. Irwin, Inc., 1961), p. 7.
3. Dan M. McGill, *Fundamentals of Private Pensions,* 3rd ed., (Homewood, IL: Richard D. Irwin Inc., 1975), p. 16.
4. Lee Willing Squier, *Old Age Dependency in the United States* (New York: Macmillan Company, 1912), p. 272.
5. McGill, p. 18.
6. *Matter of Inland Steel Co.* (1948) 77 NLRB 1.

7. *Inland Steel Company v. National Labor Relations Board,* 170 F.2d 247, 251 (1948). *Certiorari denied by the Supreme Court,* 336 U.S. 960 (1949).

8. Joint Economic Committee, "Special Study on Economic Change," *Social Security and Pensions: Programs of Equity and Security* (Washington, D.C.: Joint Economic Committee, 1980), p. 3.

9. *Ibid.,* pp. 16–17.

10. *Ibid.,* p. 4.

11. *Loc. cit.*

12. *Loc. cit.*

13. U.S., Congress, Senate, Subcommittee on Labor, Committee on Labor and Public Welfare, "Employee Benefit Security Act of 1974: Material Explaining H.R. 12906 Together with Supplemental Views (To Accompany H.R. 2)," *Legislative History of the Employee Retirement Income Security Act,* Pub. L. 93-406, 93rd Congress, 2d Session, February 25, 1974 (Washington, D.C.: U.S. Government Printing Office, 1976), p. 3295.

14. The Internal Revenue Code, as amended by ERISA, provides three alternative methods for determining the maximum allowable deduction for a pension plan in any tax year:

    1. *Individual level premium.* The employer may deduct the amount necessary to fund the remaining cost of past and current service credits distributed as a level amount, or a level percentage of compensation over the remaining future service of each participant.
    2. *Normal cost plus 10-year amortization.* The employer may deduct an amount equal to the normal cost of the plan plus any supplementary cost amortized in equal annual payments over 10 years.
    3. *Minimum funding standards.* The employer may deduct the amount necessary to satisfy ERISA's minimum funding requirements for the plan year if that amount exceeds the amounts determined under the first two methods.

    Each of these methods is subject to an overall limit, called the full-funding limitation. Contributions in excess of the deduction limits may be carried over to succeeding tax years and deducted within the limits. Moreover, where one or more employees are covered under a pension and profit-sharing or stock bonus plan of the same employer, the total deduction for contributions to all plans is generally limited to 25% of compensation.

15. For this purpose, the actual Social Security wage is not used. Instead, the wage bases are used that would have been in effect had the 1977 Amendments to the Social Security Act not been enacted.

16. See ERISA Sections 4022 and 4044 for more information on guaranteed benefits and the allocation of assets of a terminated plan to pay those benefits.

17. "ASPA-BNA Survey No. 39—Retirement Policies and Programs," *BNA Pension Reporter,* No. 276 (February 4, 1980), p. R-1.

18. A Hewitt Associates survey of salaried employee benefits (1981).

19. Donald Moffitt, "Comparing Costs of Life Insurance is Easier Than You May Think And It Can Save You Money," *The Wall Street Journal,* (January 15, 1979), p. 40, column 1.

THREE

BACKGROUND INFORMATION: ACTUARIAL PRINCIPLES

In order to appreciate the issues involved in accounting for pension costs, it is necessary to understand how pension costs are determined. For a defined benefit pension plan, current and future costs are estimated by an actuary through the use of various statistical, financial, mathematical, and other techniques in a process called an actuarial valuation. For defined contribution plans, actuarial techniques are not used to determine contributions; instead contributions are fixed under the terms of the plan.

This chapter discusses the general nature of pension costs and the actuarial assumptions and methods used in estimating these costs for defined benefit pension plans.

THE GENERAL NATURE OF PENSION COSTS

The ultimate cost of a pension plan—total benefits and expenses paid out less pension fund earnings and employee contributions—cannot be exactly determined while the plan is operating since the ultimate benefits for active employees are unknown and, once employees are retired, the duration of benefit payments is also unknown. Accordingly, pension costs must be estimated. The estimation methodology is complex and based on a number of factors:

- Plan provisions,

- Nature and experience of the plan membership,

- Actuarial assumptions, and

- Actuarial methods.

Actuarial assumptions refer to a number of factors (mortality, interest, etc.) considered by the actuary when estimating the total benefits ultimately to be paid by a plan and the present value of these benefits. The estimated present value of future benefits is then allocated as an annual cost to past, current, and future years by an actuarial cost method.

THE ACTUARIAL PRESENT VALUE CONCEPT

Basic to actuarial determinations of pension cost is the present value concept. This concept permits a value at any future point in time to be expressed as an equivalent value at the present time under a given set of conditions. It also permits a series of financial transactions over a period of time to be expressed as a single value at any point of time.

The use of the present value concept for pension benefits normally involves several factors in addition to the time value of invested funds. For instance, in determining the present value of a pension benefit to be paid 40 years in the future, an actuary considers such factors as:

- The probability that the plan member will neither die nor terminate but will continue in active employment for the next 40 years until retirement,

- The employee's salary throughout his career or at retirement,

- The probability that the employee will survive to receive each successive month's annuity payment assuming he does reach retirement, and

- The investment return that money placed in the pension fund can be expected to earn over the period from the present until the retiree receives his last payment.

Having attached a probability or numerical value to each of these factors, the actuary combines them mathematically to determine the present value of the future plan benefit.

ACTUARIAL ASSUMPTIONS

Actuarial assumptions are a basic element in the calculation of present values of future plan benefits.

Mortality

Since pension benefits are generally not paid unless the employee lives to retirement, and may cease with the death of a retired employee, an actuarial assumption contemplating mortality rates of employees (and of their co-annuitants in the case of joint and survivorship options) is a consideration in the determination of pension costs. Making allowances for future mortality is sometimes referred to as discounting for mortality. The mortality rates used by the actuary in measuring the present value of a plan's benefits may be based on the experience of plan members, but are most often based on published studies of the mortality experience of large groups of annuitants.

Employee Turnover

An assumption is also made for the rates of future employee turnover, since termination of employment before retirement age generally reduces or eliminates benefits that would otherwise accrue, thereby reducing pension costs. Studies made of turnover rates usually involve recognition of the effects of age, sex, length of employment, and type of work. Making allowance for future employment severance is called discounting for turnover.

Retirement Age

When plans permit retirement at a date other than the normal retirement age, i.e., at either an early retirement date or a deferred retirement date, assumptions about the number of employees who will retire at various ages may be needed. However, in some plans the benefits for early retirement are adjusted to provide amounts that are equivalent actuarially, to those at normal retirement age. It is then frequently assumed that all employees will retire at normal retirement age. On the other hand, many plans provide subsidized early retirement benefits. The existence of liberal early retirement provisions and the increased number of employees taking advantage of these provisions has increased the importance of the retirement age assumption for these plans.

Salary Scales

When benefits are keyed to future salary rates, as in a percentage-of-compensation formula, assumptions may be made about future salary levels. This is essential in the case of a final pay plan, where all benefits are generally related to an employee's highest earnings for a limited period of years before retirement. The salary scale assumption takes into account future expectations of inflation, merit increases (promotion or seniority), and productivity. The extent to which each of the three components is included—or excluded—in the salary assumption depends on the nature of the plan membership and the judgment of the plan sponsor and its actuary.

Interest Rate

Monies available to provide benefits result not only from contributions but from the income earned on investment of fund assets. Recognition of future fund income is called discounting for interest.

Other Assumptions

Additional actuarial assumptions may have to be made, depending on the provisions of the plan. Thus, where plans provide for disability or death benefits, or contain features dependent on marital status or changes in a cost-of-living index or Social Security benefits, appropriate assumptions are needed as to future events with respect to these conditions.

ACTUARIAL COST METHODS

Once the present value of plan benefits has been determined, an actuarial cost method is used to assign the actuarial present value as cost to past, current, and future years.

When a plan valuation is made, the portion of cost assigned to employee service in the current year is called *normal cost*. The portion of cost assigned to years of employee service prior to the valuation of the plan is called *past service cost*.[1] Although most actuarial cost methods identify past service cost for separate amortization, some cost methods assign all costs to years subsequent to each plan valuation. The portion of total cost not assigned to the current year's normal cost or to past service cost represents costs which will be assigned as normal cost to future years.

Classification of Cost Methods

Actuarial cost methods fall into two general categories:

- Accrued benefit cost methods, sometimes called "unit credit," "unit purchase," "step-rate," or "single premium" methods, and

- Projected benefit cost methods, sometimes called "level cost" or "level premium" cost methods.

In the past, a classification of cost methods generally included two other methods—the terminal funding and the pay-as-you-go methods. Under terminal funding, pension costs are not recognized until the date of an employee's retirement. At that time, a "fund" is established that is actuarially equivalent to all payments expected to be made to the retiree under the pension plan. Under the pay-as-you-go method, costs are recognized at the time benefits are paid to retired employees. Neither of these methods is acceptable under Accounting Principles Board Opinion No. 8 (see Chapter Four), or for determining minimum funding requirements under ERISA.

Accrued Benefit Cost Methods

The accrued benefit cost methods operate on the principle that the pension benefit is or may be divided into units of benefits, each unit being related to a year of employment service. The normal cost for each year of service is the actuarial present value of the benefit unit or units assigned to that year.

The normal cost applicable to an individual employee increases with each advancing year, since it is increasingly probable that he will live, and will work for the employer, until retirement age, and there is less time to earn interest on the amount funded. The total annual cost for the group as a whole usually does not reflect the same pronounced step-up effect because of the effect of replacement, generally, of older employees upon their death or retirement by younger employees. For a mature plan population, therefore, the normal cost may be relatively uniform, while for an initially immature group, the normal cost will rise before ultimately leveling off.

The past service cost under the accrued benefit cost methods is the single sum necessary to provide for retirement benefit units for credited service for all prior years. Past service cost is usually amortized on the basis of a series of uniform payments (which recognize interest) over a specified term.

The various accrued benefit cost methods differ only in the way in which the benefit unit assigned to each year is determined. The following briefly describes each method.

Traditional Accrued Benefit Cost Method. The classic accrued benefit cost method defines the unit of benefit assigned to each year as the benefit accruing during the year under the terms of the plan. This unit of benefit can be formally expressed as the total accrued benefit earned at the end of the year less the total accrued benefit earned at the beginning of the year. Under this method then, the benefit assigned to past service at any point in time is the total accrued benefit defined by the plan.

Accrued Benefit-Salary Prorate Cost Method. The accrued benefit-salary prorate cost method defines the unit of benefit assigned to each year to be the total projected plan benefit multiplied by the ratio of the

current year's salary to the total salary expected to be earned by
the employee over his career.[2]

Accrued Benefit-Service Prorate Cost Method.   The accrued benefit-
service prorate cost method also prorates the total projected benefit to
determine each year's assigned benefit. Under this method, the
projected benefit is divided by total expected service, thus assigning a
constant unit benefit amount to each year.

Figures A and B illustrate the allocation of the projected benefit
under the three accrued benefit cost methods for an employee who
enters a typical final pay pension plan at age 25 and works until
retirement at age 65.

Figure A shows the units of benefit assigned to each year as a
percentage of the total projected benefit at age 65. Both the accrued
benefit and the accrued benefit-salary prorate cost methods assign
smaller benefit units in the early years and increasingly larger
benefit units in later years. The accrued benefit-service prorate cost
method assigns a constant benefit amount to each year. The normal
cost for a given year under each method is the actuarial present value
of the benefit unit assigned to that year.

Figure B shows the accumulation of all benefit units assigned to
prior years as a percentage of the total projected benefit at age 65. At
age 45, half-way through the employee's career, exactly one-half of
the total projected benefit has been assigned to prior years under the
accrued benefit-service prorate cost method, but only 15%–25% of the
projected benefit has been assigned under the other two methods.
The past service cost at any point in time is the actuarial present
value of the total benefit units assigned to all prior years.

Projected Benefit Cost Methods

The step-rate increases in normal costs which would occur under
the accrued benefit cost methods as an employee gets older can be
avoided by using one of the projected benefit cost methods which
assign costs in level amounts to each year of service until normal
retirement age. These methods result in higher costs in the earlier
plan years and thus lower costs in later years. A level-cost method

38

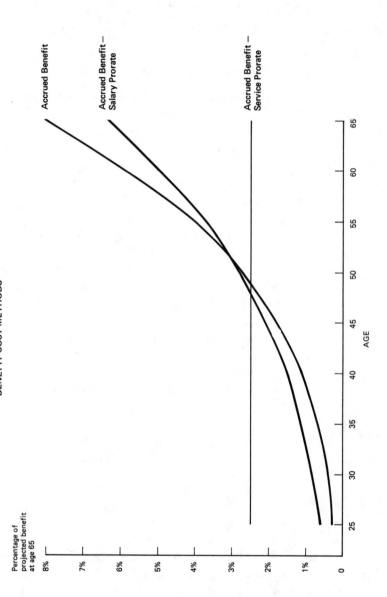

Figure A

BENEFIT ALLOCATED TO EACH AGE AS
PERCENTAGE OF TOTAL PROJECTED BENEFIT
AT AGE 65 UNDER THREE ACCRUED
BENEFIT COST METHODS

Percentage of
projected benefit
at age 65

Accrued Benefit

Accrued Benefit —
Salary Prorate

Accrued Benefit —
Service Prorate

AGE

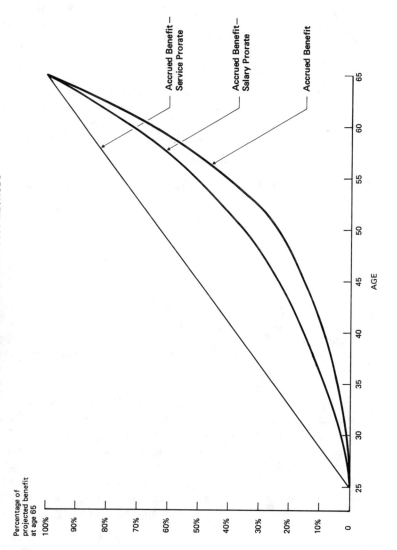

PERCENTAGE OF TOTAL PROJECTED BENEFIT AT AGE 65
WHICH HAS BEEN ALLOCATED AT EACH AGE
UNDER THREE ACCRUED BENEFIT COST METHODS

Figure B

produces normal costs that are level in dollar amounts or level as a percentage of employee salaries. If level cost is determined as of the age the employee could have entered the plan had it been in existence, it is known as the *entry age normal cost method.* If level cost is determined as of an employee's current age to cover the benefits for all subsequent years, it is known as the *attained age normal cost method.*

- **Entry Age Normal Cost Method.**   Normal cost under this method is the annual amount which would have been needed to fund pension benefits over the entire service life or lives of an employee or group of employees had the current pension plan always been in effect. Depending upon which form of the entry age normal cost method is being used, normal cost can be defined for each employee as:

  - • a constant dollar amount (entry age-constant amount cost method), or
  - • a constant percentage of salary (entry age-constant percent of salary cost method).

The term "entry age" derives from the fact that cost is determined on the assumption that the plan had always been in effect, and contributions commenced when the employee entered the plan.

Past service cost under this method is the "fund" that would have been accumulated at a given valuation date if annual normal cost contributions had, in fact, been made over the entire credited service lives of employees up to that time. This past service cost is usually amortized by level payments over a fixed period of years.

A modification of this method is often used, referred to as an "entry age normal method with frozen initial liability." The first-year costs are determined in the same way as under the entry age normal method. Past service cost is not adjusted at any future time to recognize actual experience, and it is thus termed "frozen initial liability." As a result, actuarial gains and losses are recognized in determinations of future normal cost amounts. After the first year, normal cost is computed as under the aggregate method (see below), except that the unfunded portion of the frozen liability is amortized separately.

- **Individual Level Cost Method.** This method uses the level cost approach, but fixes the level cost or level rate of compensation for each employee at an amount that would spread future pension costs over the remaining future service of the employee, thus including past service cost in normal cost, rather than treating it separately. This method is also termed the individual level premium method or the individual funding to normal retirement age method.

Under this method, past service cost (not separately identified) is in effect amortized over the remaining service lives of employees. This usually results in very high costs in the early years because the past service cost associated with participants retiring in those years is amortized over a very short period. In later years, however, this method results in costs similar to those determind under the entry age normal cost method.

- *Aggregate Method.* This method is similar to the individual level cost method, except that calculations are made on a collective basis. The total cost of future pension benefits for all employees covered at the inception of the plan is spread over their average future service lives. Normal costs are usually computed as a percentage of payroll.

Because cost is determined on a collective rather than an individual basis, past service cost, though not separately determined, is amortized over the average future service lives of all employees, thus avoiding the particularly heavy early-year costs involved under the individual level cost method.

- *Attained Age Normal Method.* This method expresses normal cost as the annual amount necessary to fund future service benefits over a period beginning with the age the employee is initially covered under the plan. The attained age normal method combines some features of the accrued benefit cost method and others of the aggregate method. As under the accrued benefit cost method, benefits are divided into units applicable to past and future service, and all units applicable to years prior to the inception of the plan are treated as past service cost. The cost of benefit units for service in years after the inception of the plan, however, is spread over employees' future service lives in a manner similar to that of the aggregate method. Normal cost is usually determined as a percentage of payroll.

Although normal costs under this method tend to decline over a period of time, costs in the early plan years are generally not as high as under the aggregate method or individual level cost method.

All of the accrued and projected benefit cost methods described above are acceptable for determining annual pension expense under Accounting Principles Board Opinion No. 8. In addition, variations of these methods may also be used (e.g., the aggregate method with frozen, separately amortized, past service cost).

Comparison of Cost Methods

Figures C and D compare normal cost and past service cost under the three accrued benefit cost methods and two projected benefit cost methods (entry age-constant percent of salary and entry age-constant amount cost methods). The comparison is for a single employee covered by a typical final pay plan.

Figure C shows normal cost as a percentage of the employee's annual compensation for each age from 25 to retirement at age 65. The step-rate pattern of the accrued benefit methods is clearly shown. The entry age methods produce level or declining normal costs as a percentage of compensation.[3]

Figure D shows past service cost under each cost method as a percentage of the present value of the employee's benefit at age 65. While all of the cost methods build to the same present value at retirement, the projected benefit (entry age) cost methods produce the largest past service cost prior to retirement.

ACTUARIAL GAINS AND LOSSES

To the extent that actual experience after an actuarial valuation differs from the actuarial assumptions used in the valuation, gains or losses will arise. For example, if more employees die prior to retirement or soon after retiring than had been anticipated, total benefits payable will be smaller than anticipated, creating an actuarial gain and reducing the otherwise required contributions. The opposite situation would involve an actuarial loss.

Computing Actuarial Gain or Loss

Analyzing and computing the amount of gain or loss attributable to each actuarial assumption is more difficult than calculating

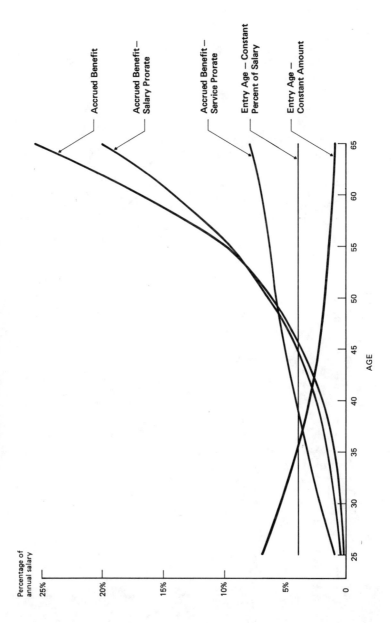

Figure C

NORMAL COST AS PERCENTAGE OF
ANNUAL SALARY UNDER VARIOUS
COST METHODS – SINGLE INDIVIDUAL

43

44

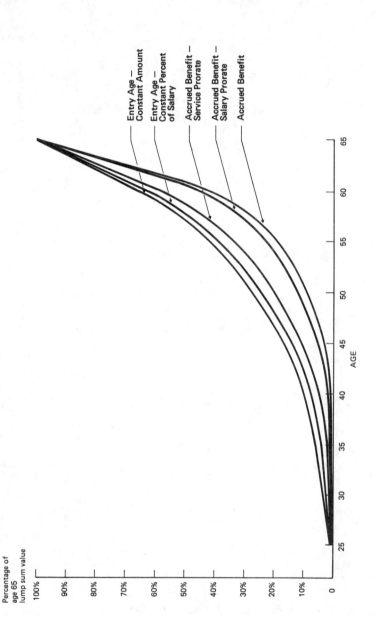

Figure D

PAST SERVICE COST AS PERCENTAGE
OF ULTIMATE LUMP SUM VALUE OF
RETIREMENT BENEFIT AT AGE 65 —
SINGLE INDIVIDUAL

Entry Age —
Constant Amount

Entry Age —
Constant Percent
of Salary

Accrued Benefit —
Service Prorate

Accrued Benefit —
Salary Prorate

Accrued Benefit

Percentage of
age 65
lump sum value

100%

90%

80%

70%

60%

50%

40%

30%

20%

10%

0

25   30   35   40   45   50   55   60   65

AGE

aggregate net gain or loss on an overall basis. As part of the annual actuarial valuation of a plan, however, the actuary will frequently make the technical computations necessary to determine the sources of gains or losses in order to compare actual experience with assumed experience for each assumption. It is necessary to make these analyses from time to time in order to decide when adjustments should be made in the assumptions to be used in the future.

In the case of actuarial cost methods that reflect gains and losses as adjustments to past service cost, the aggregate gain or loss can be determined by comparing the actual unfunded past service cost at the valuation date with the unfunded past service cost that would have existed if experience had followed the actuarial assumptions used, taking into account the actual contributions made to the fund. In the case of actuarial cost methods that reflect gains and losses in future normal costs, the aggregate gain or loss can be determined by comparing the actual unfunded future normal costs with the unfunded future normal costs that would have existed if experience had followed the actuarial assumptions, again taking into account the actual contributions made. If the expected unfunded amount exceeds the actual unfunded amount, the difference is an actuarial gain; the opposite is an actuarial loss.

Actuarial Gain or Loss Adjustment

Actuarial gains or losses may be used as adjustments to costs immediately, or averaged or spread over a period of years. The methods by which pension costs are adjusted for actuarial gains or losses are discussed below.

- *Immediate Recognition.* The first method, called immediate recognition, entails the immediate addition of an amount equal to the loss to (or subtraction of an amount equal to the gain from) the current or following year's normal cost. Where there is a significant loss, however, it can be added to the unfunded past service cost, which is almost always done when one of the accrued benefit (step-rate) cost methods is used. Current accounting policy as set forth in Accounting Principles Board Opinion No. 8 specifies that, in most situations, gains and losses should be averaged or spread instead of recognized immediately. Minimum funding requirements established by ERISA require that actuarial gains or losses be spread over 15 years in level amortization amounts. As a result, the immediate recognition method of adjusting pension costs for gains and losses is less common today than it once was.

- *Averaging.*   The second method involves averaging gains or losses over future periods. Under this method, an average of accrued net gains or losses with consideration of those expected to occur in the future, is applied to normal cost.

- *Spreading.*   The third adjustment method spreads gains and losses over future periods and is almost always used with the projected benefit cost methods (level funding). Depending on the cost method, the gain or loss is spread either by amortization over a fixed period in the same manner as past service costs or by adjusting future normal costs.

In the aggregate cost method, the spreading technique is automatically used because costs are based on the present value of all unfunded future benefits. Thus, a revised normal cost rate at any valuation date automatically spreads the adjustment over future periods. Since the past service cost is not separately determined in the computation of the normal cost rate, this method, in effect, applies the actuarial gain or loss to all future normal costs.

Under other cost methods which do not involve an aggregate calculation or a "frozen" supplemental liability (e.g., the entry age method), actuarial gains or losses are amortized over a fixed period. Thus under these methods, actuarial gains or losses must be calculated each year.

METHODS OF VALUING PLAN ASSETS

The valuation of fund assets is a principal factor in the calculation of a plan's costs and actuarial gains and losses and in the determination of any underfunding or overfunding.

In performing actuarial valuations, pension fund investment portfolios were traditionally valued at cost, thus excluding unrealized gains or losses from the calculation.

Current accounting policy as set forth in Accounting Principles Board Opinion No. 8 and legal requirements on minimum funding established by ERISA, require that unrealized appreciation and depreciation be recognized in the determination of pension cost for accounting and minimum funding purposes.

Several techniques are utilized for the gradual recognition of unrealized appreciation or depreciation. Perhaps the most popular is an averaging technique to spread unrealized appreciation or depreciation over a relatively short period such as five years.

NOTES

1. Other terminology used by actuaries in referring to past service cost includes past service liability, supplemental liability, and prior service cost. APB Opinion No. 8 distinguishes between past service cost (plan cost assigned to years prior to the inception of a plan) and prior service cost (plan cost assigned to years prior to a particular valuation of the plan, including any remaining past service cost).

2. The Internal Revenue Service has taken the position in Regulation Section 1.412 (c)(3)-1 that this method is only acceptable when used with a career average plan. On the other hand, the American Academy of Actuaries regards this method as reasonable and acceptable under certain circumstances.

3. The entry age-constant amount cost method produces a normal cost which is a constant dollar amount, and which therefore declines as a percentage of the employee's increasing annual compensation.

FOUR

ACCOUNTING PRINCIPLES

This chapter discusses highlights in the development of generally accepted accounting principles for employers' accounting for pension costs and other post-retirement benefits. Current accounting principles for pension costs (APB Opinion No. 8, FASB Statement No. 36, etc.) are briefly discussed as well as the Financial Accounting Standards Board's plan for the comprehensive re-examination of employer accounting for pension costs.

HISTORICAL DEVELOPMENT OF ACCOUNTING FOR PENSION COSTS

In the early part of this century, pensions were invariably accounted for on a pay-as-you-go basis, and the only charge to income was the amount of benefits paid to retired employees during the accounting period. Later, when formal funded pension plans were adopted and actuarial methods were created to allocate costs to past, current, and future periods, accounting questions were raised about the nature of contributions made for past service. The basic question was whether contributions for past service should be charged to retained earnings or to current expense.[1]

AICPA Statements

- **ARB No. 36.**   The AICPA issued its first pronouncement on accounting for pension costs in Accounting Research Bulletin (ARB) No. 36, in 1948. This bulletin expressed the opinion that costs of annuities based upon past service were generally incurred in contemplation of present and future services and that such costs should be allocated to current and future services. It did not, however, specify how pension costs should be recognized in the accounts.

- **ARB No. 47.**   In 1956, the AICPA issued ARB No. 47 to broaden the scope of ARB No. 36. ARB No. 47 specified how past service cost should be accounted for and recognized the concept of vested benefits. It expressed a preference for full accrual of pension costs over the remaining service lives of employees covered by a plan, generally on the basis of actuarial calculations. ARB No. 47 took the position that past service cost should be charged off over a reasonable period on a systematic and rational basis that would not distort operating results in any one year.[2] It was also noted that actuarial cost methods used for funding purposes may be appropriately used for accounting purposes but the accrual of costs under a pension plan should not necessarily be dependent on funding arrangements or governed by a strict legal interpretation of the obligations under the plan.[3]

CURRENT ACCOUNTING PRINCIPLES FOR PENSION COSTS

APB Opinion No. 8: In November 1966, the AICPA's Accounting Principles Board (APB) issued Opinion No. 8, "Accounting for the Cost of Pension Plans," with the objective of eliminating inappropriate fluctuations in the amount of annual provisions for pension cost.

APB Opinion No. 8 better defined the accounting treatment for pension costs by:

- Increasing the minimum required annual provision for pension cost to include a supplementary provision for vested benefits, if applicable.

- Requiring that actuarial gains and losses and unrealized appreciation and depreciation be recognized in the computation of the annual provision in a consistent manner that reflects the long-range nature of pension cost and avoids giving undue weight to short-term market fluctuations.

• Regarding pay-as-you-go and terminal funding as unacceptable because these methods give no recognition to pension costs until the employee retires.

Other provisions of APB Opinion No. 8 are described below:

• **Minimum Annual Provision.**   APB Opinion No. 8 provides for a minimum annual provision for pension cost equal to the total of:

   • • Normal cost.
   • • An amount equivalent to interest on unfunded prior service cost.[4]
   • • A supplemental provision for vested benefits, if required.[5]

• **Maximum Annual Provision.**   The *maximum annual provision* for pension cost provided for in APB Opinion No. 8 is equal to the total of:

   • • Normal cost.
   • • 10% of past service cost[6] at inception of the plan and of increases or decreases in prior service cost arising from plan amendments (in each case until fully amortized).
   • • Interest equivalents on differences between provisions and amount funded.

• **Actuarial Cost Methods.**   APB Opinion No. 8 identifies actuarial cost methods which result in an appropriate annual provision for pension cost. An explanation of the cost methods is provided in Chapter Three.

• **Actuarial Gains and Losses.**   Under APB Opinion No. 8, adjustments required to reflect actual experience must be consistently recognized to reflect the long-range nature of pension costs. Except in specified situations (e.g., plant closings), actuarial gains and losses are to be spread or averaged rather than immediately recognized. The latter course is considered undesirable because of the possibility of wide fluctuations in annual pension expense. Ten to twenty years is considered a reasonable period over which to spread actuarial gains and losses when spreading is accomplished by separate amortization rather than by the routine application of the actuarial cost method used. APB Opinion No. 8 also requires recognition of unrealized appreciation or depreciation in the value of equity investments.

• **Disclosures.**   APB Opinion No. 8 calls for specific disclosures on pension costs in the financial statements or notes, and the Securities and Exchange Commission has required certain additional *disclosures.*

PENSION PLAN DISCLOSURE REQUIREMENTS UNDER APB
OPINION NO. 8 AND UNDER RULES AND REGULATIONS OF THE
SECURITIES AND EXCHANGE COMMISSION

APB OPINION NO. 8- Paragraph 46

1. A statement that such plans exist, identifying or describing the employee groups covered.
2. A statement of the company's accounting and funding policies.
3. The provision for pension cost for the period.
4. The excess, if any, of the actuarially computed value of vested benefits over the total of the pension fund and any balance sheet pension accruals, less any pension prepayments or deferred charges.
5. Nature and effect of significant matters affecting comparability for all periods presented, such as changes in accounting methods (actuarial cost method, amortization of past and prior service cost, treatment of actuarial gains and losses, etc.), changes in circumstances (actuarial assumptions, etc.), or adoption or amendment of a plan.

SEC-Rule 3-16 (g) of Regulation S-X[7]

1. A brief description of the essential provisions of any employee pension or retirement plan and of the accounting and funding policies related thereto.
2. The estimated cost of the plan for each period for which an income statement is presented.
3. The excess, if any, of the actuarially computed value of vested benefits over the total of the pension fund and any balance sheet pension accruals, less any pension prepayments or deferred charges.
4. If a plan has not been fully funded or otherwise provided for, the estimated amount that would be necessary to fund or otherwise provide for the past service cost of the plan as of the date most recently determined.
5. A statement of the nature and effect of significant matters affecting comparability of pension costs for any periods for which income statements are presented.

Special Situations

- **Death and Disability Benefits.** The benefits to be considered in calculating the annual cost of a pension plan are ordinarily the retirement benefit payments. Generally, death and disability benefits should be considered as part of the benefits provided by the pension plan only if they are an integral part of the benefits provided by the plan.

- **Deferred Compensation Contracts.**   Accounting for deferred compensation contracts is generally governed by the provisions of paragraphs 6, 7, and 8 of APB Opinion No. 12. APB Opinion No. 8, however, also refers to these contracts, indicating that its provisions are applicable if the contracts taken together are equivalent to a pension plan. The principal difference is that APB Opinion No. 12 requires accrual of deferred compensation generally over the remaining service lives of individual employees, whereas APB Opinion No. 8 permits accrual of pension costs over varying time periods due to the alternative treatments allowed in providing for past service cost.

- **Defined Contribution Plans.**   The periodic cost of a defined contribution plan is usually appropriately measured by the amount of contribution determined by the formula specified in the plan. In other words, the actual contribution accrued with respect to the accounting period is the proper amount of the current charge to expense. For certain union-negotiated plans (i.e., *multiemployer plans*) there has been some question as to whether they should be treated as defined contribution or defined benefit plans. For example, if a plan provides both a formula for plan contributions and stated plan benefits, and the benefit levels are to be maintained regardless of the contribution level, the plan should be treated as a defined benefit plan with the current charge to expense computed actuarially. In this regard, the Ninth Circuit Court of Appeals held in the *Connolly v. PBGC*[8] case that the operating engineers' pension plan is a defined benefit plan subject to the termination insurance provisions of ERISA.

- **Plant Closings.**   Actuarial gains and losses should be recognized immediately if they arise from a single occurrence not directly related to the operation and not in the ordinary course of an employer's business, such as a plant closing. There are numerous questions as to how this specific treatment should apply to plant closings and other reductions in an employer's work force.

- **Business Combinations.**   Accounting for pensions in business combinations is governed by APB Opinion No. 16, which recognizes two types of business combinations and prescribes the appropriate accounting treatments described below.

  - • **Pooling of Interest Method.**   Use of the pooling of interest method is restricted to business combinations that meet prescribed conditions related to the attributes of the combining companies, the manner of combining interests, and the absence of certain planned future transactions. This method is intended to present as a single interest two or more common stockholder interests which were previously independent and the combined rights and risks represented by these interests. For the most part, this is achieved by combining the recorded assets and liabilities (which are adjusted to the same basis of accounting), as well as the stockholders' equity of the separate companies.

- • **Purchase Method.**   Accounting for a business combination by the purchase method generally follows historical cost accounting principles. Under this method, the greater of the following amounts should be recorded as a liability:

  (1) The accrued pension cost computed in conformity with the accounting policies of the acquiring corporation for one or more of its pension plans, or

  (2) The excess, if any, of the actuarially computed value of vested benefits over the amount of the pension fund.

FASB Interpretation No. 3: After ERISA was enacted, there was concern about its impact on accounting for pension costs. As a temporary measure, the FASB issued Interpretation No. 3. "Accounting for the Cost of Pension Plans Subject to the Employee Retirement Income Security Act of 1974, an Interpretation of APB Opinion No. 8."

Interpretation No. 3 states that the FASB does not believe that ERISA creates a legal obligation for unfunded pension costs that warrants recognition as an accounting liability. Generally, only the amount currently required to be funded under ERISA should be recognized as a liability.

The FASB Interpretation also indicates that when there is convincing evidence that a pension plan will be terminated and the liability on termination will exceed fund assets and related prior accruals, the excess liability should be accrued. Further, if the amount of the excess liability cannot be reasonably determined, disclosure of the circumstances should be made in the notes to the financial statements, including an estimate of the possible range of the liability. Recently issued FASB Technical Bulletin 81-3 generally calls for similar treatment when an employer withdraws from a multiemployer plan.

FASB STATEMENT NO. 36—FINANCIAL ACCOUNTING STANDARDS FOR THE DISCLOSURE OF PENSION INFORMATION

This statement is an interim measure, pending completion of the FASB's comprehensive re-examination of employer accounting for pension costs. FASB Statement No. 36 is effective for annual financial statements for fiscal years beginning after December 15, 1979 and for a complete set of financial statements for interim periods within those fiscal years issued after June 30, 1980.

The disclosures called for in this FASB statement replace the APB Opinion No. 8 requirement to disclose the excess, if any, of vested benefits over plan assets and any balance sheet pension accruals. The FASB did not address modifications to methods of computing annual provisions for pension costs. The new disclosures are:

• The actuarial present value of accumulated plan benefits.

• The actuarial present value of vested plan benefits.

• The date as of which the benefit information was determined.

• The assumed interest rate assumption used to determine the above.

• The plan's net assets available for benefits.

These amounts are to be determined in accordance with the requirements for the plan's financial statements that are prescribed in FASB Statement No. 35.

Accumulated plan benefits are defined in FASB Statement No. 35 as those future benefit payments attributable under the plan's provisions to employee's service rendered prior to the benefit valuation date. Future salary changes are not to be considered; future years of service are to be considered only in determining employees' expected eligibility for particular types of benefits, (e.g., early retirement, death, and disability benefits).

To measure the actuarial present value, assumptions are to be used to adjust those accumulated plan benefits to reflect the time value of money (through discounts for interest) and the probability of payment (by taking into account the probability of death, disability, withdrawal, or retirement) between the benefit valuation date and the expected date of payment. An assumption of an ongoing plan is to underlie those assumptions.

Assumed rates of return used to discount the accumulated plan benefits reflect the expected rates of return on plan investments applicable to the periods for which payment of benefits is deferred. Selection of the assumed rate of return is a matter of judgment involving the consideration of various factors including:

• Rates of return expected from investments currently held or available in the marketplace,

• Rates of return expected from the reinvestment of actual returns from those investments, and

• The investment policy of the plan including the diversity of investments currently held and expected to be held in the future.

Where accumulated benefit information, calculated in accordance with FASB Statement No. 35, is not available for compliance with FASB Statement No. 36, disclosure should be made in accordance with the requirements of APB Opinion No. 8 prior to amendment (i.e., the excess of the actuarially computed value of vested benefits over the total pension fund and any balance sheet pension accruals, less any pension prepayments or deferred charges). The employer must also disclose the reason why the information required by FASB Statement No. 36 is not provided. FASB Statement No. 36 does not affect any other provisions of APB Opinion No. 8.

FASB COMPREHENSIVE PROJECT EXAMINING ACCOUNTING FOR PENSION COSTS

There are many issues central to accounting for pension costs that the FASB has not yet addressed, including:

• Whether or not a pension plan "obligation" should be recorded as an accounting liability on the sponsoring company's balance sheet.

• How a pension obligation should be measured.

- Whether the expense provision should continue to be measured in accordance with the provisions of APB Opinion No. 8.

Questions also arise as to the relationship between expense measurement and measurement of an obligation, between accounting and funding requirements, and comparability among companies. These issues and others are discussed in Chapter Five.

The timing and scope of the FASB's overall project to re-examine accounting for pension costs are:

- A discussion memorandum covering only the basic issues was published in the first quarter of 1981.

- A document that contains the FASB's tentative conclusions on those basic issues and discusses additional issues is scheduled to be issued in early 1982.

- An exposure draft and later a final statement of financial reporting standards is scheduled to be issued covering both sets of issues in 1983.

CURRENT ACCOUNTING FOR OTHER POST-RETIREMENT BENEFITS

Costs of post-retirement benefits provided under pension plans are governed by APB Opinion No. 8. There are no applicable accounting pronouncements when the benefits (primarily health and death benefits) are provided outside pension plans. The costs are accounted for in a variety of ways:

- On a pay-as-you-go basis—expense is charged at the time the benefits are paid.

- On a terminal funding basis—at the time an employee terminates his service an amount is charged to expense equivalent to that needed to fund the expected future benefits.

- On an accrual basis—the costs are charged to expense over the employees' working years based on an actuarial cost method.

The most common accounting practice is pay-as-you-go expensing with no advance accrual.

In July 1979 the FASB issued an Exposure Draft, "Disclosure of Pension and Other Post-Retirement Benefit Information." For the first time, disclosure requirements would have been extended to post-retirement benefits other than pensions. Specifically, the Exposure Draft would have required the disclosure of the following information:

- A description of the benefits.

- A description of the accounting policies used with respect to the benefits.

- The cost of the benefits which were included in determining net income for the period to which the disclosure relates.

The Exposure Draft only called for these disclosures and did not propose to establish accounting principles concerning the measurement of costs.

Although the FASB did not institute these disclosure requirements, the subject of post-retirement benefits is included in the FASB's overall project to re-examine accounting for pension costs. The FASB apparently believes that these benefits are significant and similar enough to pensions to include them in the project.

NOTES

1. Felix Pomeranz, Gordon P. Ramsey and Richard M. Steinberg, *Pensions—An Accounting and Management Guide,* (New York: Ronald Press, 1976), p. 84

2. American Institute of Certified Public Accountants, *Accounting Research Bulletin No. 47, Accounting for the Cost of Pension Plans,* (New York: AICPA, 1956), paragraphs 5 and 7.

3. *Ibid,* paragraph 5.

4. The term *unfunded prior service cost* includes unfunded past service cost and unfunded increases in past service cost arising from plan amendments. Normal cost is generally funded on a current basis, in conformance with past and present Internal Revenue Code requirements for qualified plans. In such cases normal cost is not included in unfunded prior service cost.

5. The supplemental provision for vested benefits is described in Paragraph 17a. of APB Opinion No. 8.

6. This includes an interest factor and therefore it will take longer than ten years to amortize these amounts.

7. SEC-Rule 3-16(q) of Regulation S-X was deleted in 1980 to avoid duplication with FASB Statement No. 36, published earlier that year. We are including this data for historical, comparative purposes.

8. *Connolly v. PBGC* (CA-9 rev'g DC Cal) 581 F2d 729.

FIVE

ISSUES AND ALTERNATIVES

INTRODUCTION: OVERVIEW OF CURRENT CONCERNS

The question of whether present accounting practice accurately and meaningfully presents the financial effect of an employer's pension plan responsibilities is receiving significant attention. Of particular concern is the presentation and measurement of so-called unfunded pension liabilities. Some suggest that the accounting and actuarial treatment of pension liabilities is a masterpiece of confusion, since equally acceptable actuarial cost methods can result in widely differing patterns of cost recognition for similar economic circumstances. Furthermore, it is asserted that there is too much latitude in the application of actuarial assumptions.[1,2]

Interest exists in comparing the financial impact of pension obligations on various plan sponsors. However, financial analysts are frustrated because they believe there are no standards available for making the comparison.[3] In other words, it is felt by some that current financial statement disclosures on pensions do not tell investors what they need to know. Nonetheless, a recent study indicated that reported pension data affects stock prices.[4] On the other hand, another recent study found no apparent relationship between a plan sponsor's "unfunded liability" and its price/earnings ratio.[5]

In November 1980, the then Chairman of the Securities and Exchange Commission voiced concern over pension disclosures in registrants' financial statements. He indicated that disclosures required by FASB Statement No. 36 are not indicative of an employer's future pension expenditures. Moreover, if in reviewing this year's (1980) financial statements the SEC staff finds the disclosure to be inadequate, it may recommend that the SEC consider implementing additional requirements until the FASB completes its comprehensive pension project. He urged registrants to expand their disclosures, where necessary, to assist users of financial statements in understanding the information.[6]

Although there is concern about unfunded pension liabilities, many corporate executives and experts in the benefits field believe that the problem is greatly exaggerated.[7] They contend that the major issue is whether plan sponsors are going concerns that can continue to meet their annual commitments to make pension plan contributions.[8] Moreover, computing ratios of unfunded liabilities to earnings or net worth is futile, because knowing the amount of a company's unfunded liability is useless unless other information such as the actuarial cost method, the choice of actuarial assumptions, and the actual pension contribution is understood.

This chapter identifies several of the major issues regarding accounting for pension costs and discusses various alternative treatments. The issues discussed are:

- Should an obligation for pension costs be recognized as an accounting liability on the sponsoring company's balance sheet?

- If an obligation is recognized or disclosed how should it be measured?

- How should actuarial assumptions be selected in determining the obligation?

- Should the obligation be recorded (or disclosed) net of plan assets?

- How should assets be valued?

- How should the debit corresponding to any recorded obligation be reported?

- How should the annual expense provision be determined?

- If no obligation is recorded, should the current expense rules be changed?

- If an obligation is recorded, should expense be related to the obligation determination?

- What additional disclosures should be made?

- Other issues—

  - • multiemployer plans
  - • plant closings
  - • foreign plans
  - • termination indemnities
  - • other post-retirement benefits

ISSUE: SHOULD AN OBLIGATION FOR PENSION COSTS BE RECOGNIZED AS AN ACCOUNTING LIABILITY ON THE SPONSORING COMPANY'S BALANCE SHEET?

One of the major issues in accounting for pension costs involves the basic question of the existence of an accounting liability. The FASB defines accounting liabilities as probable future sacrifices of economic benefits arising from present obligations to transfer assets in the future as a result of past events. The obligation must require settlement at or upon a specified date or event; the enterprise should have little or no discretion to avoid settlement, and the event giving rise to the obligation must already have occurred.[9]

Unfortunately, this definition does not provide sufficient guidelines for determining whether a pension obligation should be recorded and, if so, how the obligation should be measured.

Record no Liability

Current accounting practice does not require a sponsoring company to record a liability for the pension benefits of an ongoing plan.

- Pension benefits are normally an obligation of the plan rather than the sponsor. ERISA's requirement that plan assets be held in trust and its establishment of the plan as a separate accounting entity, along with the Internal Revenue Code's general prohibition on reversion of plan assets to the sponsor, all point to the plan's status as a separate legal entity responsible for the satisfaction of pension obligations. The only potential liability of the sponsor, the "contingent" employer liability discussed in Chapter Two, does not meet the definition of an accounting liability until the event resulting in an obligation—plan termination has occurred.

- Even if it were agreed that pension benefits represent an accounting liability of the sponsor, they should not be recorded on the balance sheet in view of problems inherent in their measurement.

- Adoption of a pension plan, past service pension improvements, and increases for current retirees are granted primarily to encourage current employees to provide future services. The employer's commitment is similar to the effect of wage and salary increases. All are essentially provided to purchase future productive effort and, accordingly, immediate liability recognition would not be appropriate. Moreover, charging to income all of the cost of a past service improvement in the year it is granted could adversely impact the establishment and improvement of defined benefit plans and could significantly affect the collective bargaining process.

- Current accounting principles adequately reflect the going concern concept which is applicable to most plan situations. So long as an entity continues as a going concern, the obligation for pension costs will be fully reflected through the annual expense provision, and no additional costs will be incurred.

- Sophisticated readers of financial statements do not focus attention on any one measure of pension obligation, but rather on the annual charge to income. Disclosure of the expense provision provides financial statement users with the ability to make comparisons within an industry and with sufficient information to evaluate the financial impact of pensions on the sponsor's income statement.

Record a Liability

Arguments for recording an obligation for pension costs are:

- The obligation meets the definition of a liability as set forth by the FASB. The obligation will be satisfied by future transfers of assets, it will require settlement on or upon a future date or event, the sponsor has little or no discretion to avoid settlement, and the event giving rise to the obligation—the rendering of service by participant—has already occurred.

- On a going concern basis, which is an assumption basic to financial statement presentations, there is no question that retirement benefits will ultimately be paid to participants.

- Measurement techniques are available, and have long been used, to provide a reasonable estimate of the amount of the obligation.

ISSUE: IF AN OBLIGATION IS RECOGNIZED (OR DISCLOSED) HOW SHOULD IT BE MEASURED?

The following discussion examines some of the major alternatives for defining and recognizing an accounting liability for pensions:

- PBGC guaranteed benefits;

- Vested benefits;

- Accumulated benefits;

- Benefits at risk;

- Pro-rata allocation of projected benefits; and

- Prior service liability produced by the actuarial cost method used for expense or funding purposes.

Although the alternatives are presented in terms of liability recognition, they are also generally applicable to the question of what amount(s) should be disclosed in financial statement footnotes if no liability, or another liability measure, is recorded.

PBGC Guaranteed Benefits

As discussed more fully in Chapter Two, the Pension Benefit Guaranty Corporation (PBGC) provides termination insurance covering vested basic benefits subject to certain plan limitations. There is support for recognizing any unfunded PBGC guaranteed benefits as an accounting liability, up to a ceiling of 30% of the sponsor's net worth (for single employer plans), under the rationale that the "contingent" employer liability under ERISA establishes a legal obligation for the sponsor to provide these benefits. They are payable whether or not the plan continues in existence.

Vested Benefits

Vested benefits are generally defined as benefits for which entitlement to payment is not contingent upon the participant's continued service. Thus, vested benefits include:

- The value of current and future benefits payable to retirees, beneficiaries, and plan members who have terminated service with vested rights as of the determination date, and

- The value of benefits which would be payable to active members in the future, assuming they all terminated on the determination date.

Therefore, the vested benefit of an active member is related to service rendered and salary earned up to the date of determination and the member's vesting percentage under the plan's vesting schedule as of that date.

Proponents of the use of vested benefits as the measure of a sponsor's liability point out that:

- The plan is likely to continue to exist, and the sponsor will be obligated to provide all vested benefits, regardless of any future change in an individual's employment relationship. Thus, the fulfillment of vesting requirements is the event that triggers the sponsor's obligation to pay the benefits.

- For most plans, no additional calculations would be required. The value of vested benefits must presently be calculated for both Form 5500, Schedule B, and for financial statement purposes under FASB Statement Nos. 35 and 36. In contrast, the calculation of PBGC guaranteed benefits would involve additional complex and expensive termination priority allocations in accordance with Section 4044 of ERISA.

Accumulated Benefits

The concept of accumulated benefits takes the going concern approach to liability measurement one step beyond vested benefits. The present value of accumulated benefits includes all vested benefits plus the value of active members' non-vested benefits earned at the determination date.

The accumulated benefits of an active member are related to service rendered and salary levels to the date of determination, the member's vesting percentage under the plan's vesting schedule as of that date, *and* the probability that the member will remain employed from year to year and increase his vesting percentage. Determining the present value of such benefits requires the use of assumptions for withdrawal, disability, and retirement, as well as the mortality and interest assumptions.

Those supporting use of the present value of accumulated benefits as the measure of a sponsor's pension accounting liability make the following arguments:

- The event which obligates the sponsor to pay is the rendering of service resulting in benefit accrual under the plan.

- Use of the present value of accumulated benefits will result in symmetry between plan and company financial statements.

- For most plans, no additional calculations would be needed, since the calculations are required under FASB Statement Nos. 35 and 36 and for reporting on Form 5500, Schedule B.

Benefits at Risk

Benefits at risk represent the potential plan liability at a given date, assuming all participants are fully vested. The present value of benefits at risk as of a date of determination includes all vested benefits, plus the value of earned non-vested benefits of all active plan members, assuming each member is 100% vested.

The benefits at risk of an active member is, therefore, related to service rendered and salary levels to the determination date and an assumed 100% vesting percentage under the plan. Supporting rationale for use of this measure as a sponsor's liability include:

- The event which obligates the sponsor to pay the benefit is the rendering of service resulting in benefit accrual under the plan.

- The IRS requires that non-vested accrued benefits be vested to the extent funded, in the event of plan termination.

- Contrary to arguments of some observers, benefits at risk is *not* the measure of benefits that would be paid assuming a plan termination and thus is consistent with a going concern approach.

Pro-Rata Allocation of Projected Benefits

A pro-rata allocation of projected benefits starts with the total benefits ultimately expected to be paid to plan participants, taking into account assumptions for future salary levels and service, as well as withdrawal, disability, retirement, and mortality. These benefits are then allocated to past and future periods. A sponsor's obligation under a pro-rata allocation method as of a date of determination includes:

• The value of current and future benefits payable to retirees, beneficiaries, and members who have terminated service with vested rights as of the determination date, and

• The value of ultimate active life benefits assigned by the allocation method to service prior to the date of determination.

Alternative methods of allocation include allocating projected benefits as a level amount per year of service or as a level percentage of total career salary.

Proponents of the use of one of the pro-rata allocation methods present the following arguments:

• Accounting obligations need not be legal obligations, but equitable or constructive obligations.

• On a going concern basis, rendering of service is the event which obligates the sponsor to pay benefits. But unlike some other methods, such as accumulated benefits, the pro-rata allocation methods reflect all pertinent assumptions, including an assumption for salary level adjustments, to produce the most realistic estimate of benefits to be paid based on service rendered to date.

• Using this approach for plans with different provisions, but providing the same ultimate benefits (e.g., flat dollar per year plan, final pay plan, and career average plan), will result in the same measure of obligation if benefit improvements are anticipated and taken into account. Under some other methods, such as accumulated benefits, amounts will differ even though the ultimate benefits under each plan are identical.

• Use of a pro-rata allocation method produces the best estimate of the obligation at any point in time. This is because the pro-rata allocation method results in a more level growth pattern of the obligation than, for example, the accumulated benefits measure which may reflect a low obligation in early years and uneven increases in the obligation in later years.

Prior Service Cost Produced by the Actuarial Cost Method Used for Expense or Funding Purposes

As previously noted in Chapter Three, actuarial cost methods are used to establish the amount and incidence of pension fund contributions or accounting expense through the allocation of total pension costs to past, present, and future periods.

Those who support use of the same actuarial cost method to determine the obligation as that used by the employer for funding or expense purposes make the following arguments:

- Comparability derived from the use of a single mandated method is illusory, because of the many variations in plan design and covered employee groups and among funding vehicles. Thus, the cost method used for expense or funding purposes is the method that properly takes into account the characteristics of a particular plan and sponsor and produces the only realistic measure of the obligation.

- The use of this measure fosters internal consistency, since the same method would be used for expense and obligation measurement.

ISSUE: HOW SHOULD ACTUARIAL ASSUMPTIONS BE SELECTED IN DETERMINING THE OBLIGATION WHETHER RECORDED OR DISCLOSED?

Assumptions for future employee turnover, death, disability, and retirement are typically used by actuaries in estimating the probability that members will become eligible to receive benefits. Assumptions for salary progression, cost of living increases, and changes in Social Security levels normally are used in estimating benefit amounts. Also, an assumption for future investment yield on pension plan assets, referred to as an interest assumption, is used to discount the expected benefit payments to the determination date in order to reflect their present value. However, not all assumptions are used with all methods for calculating pension obligations.

The following discussion deals with the quantification of those types of assumptions that are required by the various obligation measures. The choice of quantitative value for assumptions significantly influences the amount of the obligation. For example, in the case of the interest assumption, a 1% increase in the interest assumption (e.g., from 7% to 8%) will frequently result in a 10% or greater decrease in the present value of accumulated benefits. For more information on the impact of assumptions see Chapter Seven which presents our modeling analyses.

Alternatives for selecting actuarial assumptions include:

1. Mandating the use of specific values,

2. Requiring the same assumptions as are used for expense purposes, and

3. Requiring the use of explicit assumptions.

Mandating Specific Values

One approach is to mandate specific quantitative values for certain assumptions such as mortality and interest and, if other assumptions are required for the calculation, precise methodology for selecting them would be established. Proponents of this approach point to the need for symmetry among companies, in order to foster comparability of financial statements. Another major argument for this approach is that it removes most, if not all, subjectivity from the calculations. Two means of mandating specific assumptions would be to require use of assumptions inherent in the cost of an insurance company annuity, or to use the mortality and interest assumptions specified by the PBGC for use in plan termination liability calculations.

Requiring the Same Assumptions as are Used for Expense Purposes

An alternative to mandating any or all assumptions is to require the use of the same assumptions that are used for calculating pension expense. Arguments supporting this approach include the following:

- The diverse investment philosophies and experiences of sponsoring companies preclude mandating specific interest, turnover, and other assumptions.

- APB Opinion No. 8 requires the use of reasonable assumptions in measuring annual pension cost. It follows that the assumptions chosen for expense calculation are equally applicable to the measurement of the obligation, since they were selected in light of the particular characteristics of the plan and sponsor. Moreover, in a majority of situations the assumptions used for expense are identical to those used for funding, which by law are required to represent the actuary's best estimate of anticipated experience under the plan.

- The use of these assumptions would provide internal consistency between the expense and obligation amounts presented in financial statements.

- The effort and cost to calculate the obligation would normally be less than if alternative assumptions were required.

Requiring the Use of Explicit Assumptions

A third alternative is to require the use of individual assumptions reflecting the best estimate of the plan's future experience (referred to as an "explicit" approach). This contrasts with an "implicit" approach, whereby the individual assumptions do not stand alone, but when taken together, represent the actuary's best estimate of future experience. An explicit approach is generally required when calculating the present value of accumulated benefits.

Arguments in support of the explicit approach include:

- The assumptions would take into account the individual characteristics of the plan and sponsor, and

- Symmetry would be achieved between employer financial statements and plan financial statements for assumptions common to both.

ISSUE: SHOULD THE OBLIGATION BE RECORDED (OR DISCLOSED) NET OF PLAN ASSETS?

In the event that a pension obligation is recorded as a liability on the sponsor's balance sheet, it must be determined whether the "gross" obligation and the plan assets should both be recorded. The alternatives are discussed here.

Record the Obligation Net of Plan Assets

Arguments for recording the net obligation include:

- ERISA and earlier Internal Revenue Code requirements have established the plan as a legal entity separate from the sponsor. A plan's assets must be held (or insured) for the exclusive benefit of the plan participants.[10] Therefore, plan assets are not available for the sponsor's general use and consequently do not belong on the sponsor's financial statements.

- The obligation to provide the benefits to participants is a sponsor obligation only to the extent that the obligation is not covered by the plan's assets.[11] Thus, only the unfunded obligation belongs on the sponsor's financial statements.

- If both the assets and the obligation are recognized on the sponsor's balance sheet, in the event of overfunding, there would be an increase in recorded net worth when, in fact, the assets may revert to the sponsor only in the case of plan termination.[12]

Record Both the Obligation and Plan Assets

The major argument for recording gross amounts is that the magnitude of both the obligation and assets is meaningful information in evaluating an employer's financial condition. Other arguments are based on the FASB's proposed definition of assets as "probable future economic benefits obtained or controlled by a particular enterprise as a result of past transactions or events affecting the enterprise."[13] The FASB identifies three characteristics of an asset:

- "A probable future benefit exists involving a capacity, singly or in combination with other assets, to contribute directly or indirectly to future net cash inflows,

- A particular enterprise can obtain the benefit and control others' access to it, and

- The transaction or other event giving rise to the enterprise's right to or control of the benefit has already occurred."[14]

It is argued that pension plan assets have these characteristics and therefore should be recorded on the sponsor's balance sheet.

In this regard, the FASB notes that "although the ability of an enterprise to obtain the future economic benefit of an asset and to deny or control access to it by others rests generally on a foundation of legal rights, legal enforceability of a right is not an indispensable prerequisite for an enterprise to have an asset if the enterprise otherwise will probably obtain the future economic benefit involved."[15]

The established accounting convention against recording net assets and liabilities also supports the premise that the amounts should be recorded "gross."

ISSUE: HOW SHOULD ASSETS BE VALUED?

Whether the obligation and the assets are recorded (or disclosed) separately or are netted, the appropriate method of valuing the assets must be determined. Alternatives include fair value,[16] historical cost, actuarial value, or multiple methods.

Fair Value

It is argued that the trend in accounting practice is toward use of fair values. FASB Statement No. 35 prescribes the use of fair value for all plan investments other than contracts with insurance companies. The Financial Accounting Standards Board based this requirement on its belief that fair value provides the most relevant information about the resources of a plan consistent with the primary objective of the financial statements. Accordingly, it is argued that fair value is appropriate for measuring the resources available to satisfy the obligation of the sponsor under the plan.

Supporters of the use of fair value point out that it entails no additional administrative burden since fair value is presently required for use on Form 5500.

Historical Cost

Historical cost is currently used to record most assets for accounting purposes. Supporters of the use of historical cost point out that it is objective and appropriately does not recognize unrealized gains and losses.

Actuarial Value

It has long been an objective of pension plan funding and accounting to assure that short-term fluctuations in asset values do not significantly affect contribution or expense levels. Actuaries have developed asset measures such as moving average market values which smooth the effects of short-term market fluctuations. The Internal Revenue Code generally allows use of these methods for minimum funding and tax deduction purposes, provided the method takes fair market value into account.

It is argued that the same objective and methods are applicable in measuring the assets available to satisfy a sponsor's pension obligations. Because benefits are payable many years in the future, it would be misleading to financial statement users to report a widely fluctuating unfunded obligation resulting from short-term market variations in asset values.

Multiple Methods

Assets held by a pension plan are often diversified. For example, assets may be short-term investments, such as treasury notes or commercial paper; long-term fixed income type investments such as bonds, notes, debentures, mortgages; equity securities; or real estate. It is argued that the nature of an asset and the expected holding period should influence the valuation method. For example, long-term fixed income securities expected to be held to maturity should be valued on an amortized cost basis, whereas for such securities expected to be sold in the near term, fair value is a better measure.

Special Problems Related to Contracts with Insurance Companies

For many insurance company contracts, a potential valuation problem exists because only the insurance company's stated value is available. A measure of fair value, for example, usually would require additional, and often costly, calculations.

An even more basic question—whether certain insurance company contracts should be excluded from the measures of both the pension assets and the obligation—also needs to be addressed. For example, should the value of contracts for which the associated benefits are guaranteed by the insurance company be excluded from the value of pension assets with the associated benefits excluded from the obligation?

In Statement No. 35, the Financial Accounting Standards Board concluded that it did not have sufficient information to make decisions with respect to some of the special problems associated with insurance contracts. In order that the issuance of the statement not be delayed, the Board adopted the practical solution that contracts with insurance companies be presented in plan financial statements in the same manner as required by Form 5500. Allocated contracts are excluded from plan assets, and unallocated contracts are included at the insurance company's stated value.

ISSUE: HOW SHOULD THE DEBIT CORRESPONDING TO ANY RECORDED OBLIGATION BE REPORTED?

If a pension obligation is recorded in the sponsor's financial statements, it must be determined where the corresponding debit is to be reflected. Three alternatives are:

- Charge to retained earnings.
- Deferred charge.
- Direct charge to income.

This discussion only addresses the accounting treatment when a liability is first recorded—that is, upon inception of, or amendment to, a plan or adoption of new standards for accounting for pension obligations.

Charge to Retained Earnings

A charge to retained earnings reflects the premise that the pension obligation results from prior periods' business activities. Since the obligation is related to service rendered in prior periods, it is not appropriate to charge current and future periods with the related costs. The accounting literature supports direct charges to retained earnings in certain circumstances.

Deferred Charge

Supporters of deferred charge treatment hold that employers introduce and improve pension plans not to reward employees for past service, but to improve employee morale and productivity in future periods and to attract new personnel to the company. Although employees may receive benefits based on service rendered in prior periods, the related costs are properly charged in future accounting periods when the benefits to the sponsor of having established or improved the plan are realized through increased revenues. Therefore, a deferred charge should be established and amortized as charges to income over future periods.

Direct Charge to Income

There is some support for the view that it is neither appropriate to establish a deferred charge, since future periods should not be burdened with costs related to past activities, nor to charge retained earnings. Accordingly, the best approach may be to make a direct charge to income for the amount of the recorded obligation. It is further argued by analogy that the accounting profession appears to be moving toward expensing intangibles rather than treating them as assets in the vague category of deferred charges.[17] For example, the FASB concluded that research and development costs should be charged to expense, since it is impossible to measure the future benefits related to the costs with any degree of certainty. Similarly, in light of a lack of definite relationship between pension obligations and any future benefit to the sponsor, the obligations should be expensed immediately.

ISSUE: HOW SHOULD THE ANNUAL EXPENSE PROVISION BE DETERMINED?

APB Opinion No. 8 provides for a *minimum* annual expense provision for pension cost equal to the total of (1) normal cost, (2) an amount equivalent to interest on unfunded past service cost, and in some circumstances, (3) a supplemental provision for vested benefits. The *maximum* annual provision is generally the normal cost and 10% of past service costs. APB Opinion No. 8 specifies five acceptable actuarial cost methods, as well as variations of those methods.[18] Except in unusual circumstances, actuarial gains and losses are to be spread or averaged rather than accorded immediate recognition. From 10 to 20 years is considered a reasonable period over which to spread actuarial gains and losses. APB Opinion No. 8 also requires recognition of unrealized appreciation or depreciation in the value of investments on a systematic basis that avoids giving undue weight to short-term market fluctuations.

Alternative means of measuring annual expense may depend on whether or not an obligation is recorded as a liability of the sponsor.

IF NO OBLIGATION IS RECORDED, SHOULD THE CURRENT EXPENSE RULES BE CHANGED?

Current Rules Should Not be Changed

The expense provisions of APB Opinion No. 8 were based on the premise that existing actuarial cost methods provide systematic and rational allocation of pension plan costs to accounting periods. No amortization of past service costs is required, under the assumption that in the case of an ongoing plan, normal cost plus interest on the past service cost is usually adequate to pay current benefits and to accumulate an amount sufficient to cover vested benefits. In situations where this is not true, the Opinion requires a supplemental provision for vested benefits.

Those who argue that the provisions of APB Opinion No. 8 are adequate point out that the above reasoning is still applicable. The choice of methods should continue, since there is no single "correct" method of matching pension expenses to revenue. The method used by a company is best chosen by the plan sponsor with advice of an actuary in light of the characteristics of the plan and sponsor.

Current Rules Should be Changed

There has been much commentary on alleged inadequacies of APB Opinion No. 8, especially with respect to the flexibility permitted in calculating expense. It is argued that since the expense provision is frequently a significant component of financial statements, greater uniformity should be required in its calculation to permit comparison between companies.

Possible changes in the expense requirements include mandating a single actuarial method as the only acceptable means of allocating pension costs to accounting periods. Different actuarial cost methods vary the timing by which costs are recognized; some recognize a greater part of the total cost in the earlier years, some in later years, and some spread the costs evenly. Requiring all plans to determine expense using the same actuarial method would create a standard whereby the financial impact of pension costs on one company could be more effectively compared to the financial impact on another.

Another suggested change in calculating expense is to require use of a specified value for one or more of the actuarial assumptions used in expense determination. Merely prescribing a common actuarial cost method will not achieve comparability, since assumptions heavily influence the resulting amounts. The use of a prescribed value for one or more actuarial assumptions would remove what some see as undesirable subjectivity in the expense determination.

Another possible change in the expense rules would be to require symmetry with funding calculations, whereby the same actuarial cost method would be used for both purposes, and amortization of past service costs and gains or losses would be subject to ERISA's minimum funding and IRS' maximum deduction limits. The need for symmetry with amounts funded is supported by the FASB Statement of Financial Accounting Concepts No. 3 on "Elements of Financial Statements of Business Enterprises," which states that recorded expense "represents actual or expected cost outflows that have occurred or will eventuate as a result of the enterprise's ongoing or central operations during the period." This approach is generally supported by proponents of the view that neither one actuarial cost method nor the value of any assumption should be mandated in light of the importance of using methods and assumptions that are based on the specifications of the plan and on its experience.

Another suggested change is to require that costs assigned to prior periods be amortized, either in accordance with ERISA's minimum funding requirements or on some other basis. Since under ERISA past service costs must eventually be funded, there is no reason not to require amortization of such costs.

Another suggested change in requirements for calculating expense is to require the immediate recognition of gains and losses and amounts relating to changes in assumptions. Proponents of this suggestion argue that such changes directly affect the company's worth, and thus there is no reason to defer recognition of those events.

IF AN OBLIGATION IS RECORDED, SHOULD EXPENSE BE RELATED TO THE OBLIGATION DETERMINATION?

The FASB discussion memorandum and exposure drafts on elements of financial statements describe three views of financial accounting. Two of these views advocate correlation between the balance sheet and the income statement (articulated financial statements), while the third views each financial statement as independent of the other.

Annual Expense Should be Defined as the Change in the Unfunded Obligation

The first concept is the asset-liability view. Advocates of this approach describe earnings as the change in wealth or capital during a period. The measurement process focuses on the attributes of assets and liabilities; all other elements are viewed as differences between, or changes in, the measure of assets and liabilities.[19]

With respect to pension costs, annual expense would be defined as a change in the obligation net of assets. Proponents of this view would call for the immediate expensing of a change in the recorded pension obligation.

Expense Should be Related to the Obligation, But Not Necessarily be Equal to the Net Change

Another concept is the revenue-expense view. Its advocates define earnings as the net of revenue and expense. If the objective of financial accounting is seen as the measurement of the enterprise's earning power—that is, the long-term average ability of an enterprise to produce earnings—then financial accounting and earnings measurement is a process of matching costs with revenue.[20]

Under this method, the balance sheet serves as a means of documenting the items reported on the income statement. Unlike the proponents of the asset-liability view, proponents of the revenue-expense view are willing to introduce items to the balance sheet that do not strictly represent economic resources of the enterprise, such as deferred charges.[21]

With respect to pension expense, the revenue-expense method would permit treatment in accordance either with current generally accepted accounting principles or with any of a number of variations whereby a method of calculating the expense is established, and resulting deferred amounts are reflected on the balance sheet.

Expenses Should be Determined Independently of the Obligation

Finally, it is argued that there should be no forced relationship between the balance sheet and the income statement, that a more useful measure of earnings and financial position can be obtained by measuring revenues and expenses independently of assets and liabilities.[22] In its application to pension expense, this concept allows the most freedom of treatment in measuring both the obligation and the provision for periodic pension costs.

ISSUE: WHAT ADDITIONAL DISCLOSURES SHOULD BE MADE?

One of the objectives of financial reporting is to "provide information that is useful to present and potential investors and creditors and other financial statement users in making investment, credit, and related decisions. The information should be comprehensible to those who have a reasonable understanding of business and economic activities and are willing to study the information with reasonable diligence."[23] A recent study conducted to determine if the market utilizes the information on unfunded pension liabilities disclosed in financial statement footnotes, concluded that the information was not being used to evaluate stock value.[24] Another study, an informal survey of corporate annual reports, also concluded that Wall Street apparently is not using pension data.[25] Both studies conclude that the pension data is not being used because the data as currently reported are inadequate.

The FASB felt that there was a need for some improvement of the disclosure requirements of APB Opinion No. 8, and issued FASB Statement No. 36. (See Chapter Four for a discussion of the requirements of APB Opinion No. 8 and FASB Statement No. 36.)

The FASB received numerous comment letters on the Exposure Draft of Statement No. 36. The letters indicated that there is broad support for some change in the disclosure requirements, but wide disagreement regarding what should be done. Some respondents hold that the entire focus of the disclosure requirements is misplaced. Others point to a lack of consistency and comparability in the amounts disclosed, while others emphasize that not enough information is disclosed.

Some who believe that the entire focus of the disclosure requirements is wrong argue that the problem with current disclosure is that it is widely misunderstood. One respondent points out, for example, that a financial statement user who looks for an indication of the plan's future ability to sustain payment of pension benefits would be misled by the disclosure of information such as the present value of accumulated benefits and the fair market value of plan assets. Since no continuing pension plan can pay all future benefits with current assets, any statement or information which may be interpreted to so indicate should be considered at least misleading. It was further argued that only the assessment of the future ability to pay benefits is relevant, that is, the rate of accrual of pension plan costs and the rate at which the sponsor is providing for these costs.[26]

Some who would like to see greater consistency and comparability point to the flexibility now permitted in actuarial calculations as the root of the problem. They argue that only one method of calculation should be acceptable and that there should be uniformity in actuarial assumptions and amortization periods. Where uniformity in calculation is not feasible, there should at least be more information disclosed, such as the cost method, the actuarial assumptions, and the amortization periods.[27]

Although many respondents agree that not enough data is provided to make current disclosures effective, the additional information called for varies considerably.[28]

OTHER ISSUES

Multiemployer Plans

As noted in Chapter Four, there is uncertainty as to whether some multiemployer plans should be treated as defined contribution or defined benefit plans. In this regard, *Connolly v. PBGC*,[29] held that the operating engineer's pension plan was a defined benefit plan, thereby raising issues regarding accounting for other, similar multiemployer plans.

If sponsors are required to record or disclose some measure of obligations related to single employer plans, should the same be required for multiemployer plans? If so, problems arise because an

actuary must separately determine obligations related to each participating employer. One alternative might be to use some measure of
the employer withdrawal liability (briefly discussed in Chapter
Two). Also, the question of how to determine the assets corresponding to any such obligation would need to be addressed. Similar
allocation questions would arise in determining annual expense.

Plant Closings

The Task Force on Pension Plans and Pension Costs of the
American Institute of Certified Public Accountants recently
addressed the question of accounting for vested pension benefits
existing or arising when a plant is closed or a business segment is
discontinued. The basic question is whether, when a plant closes,
vested benefits which have not yet been expensed should be charged
to income immediately or amortized over future periods.

An argument supporting immediate expensing is based on the
premise that plant closings are not part of the ordinary course of
business; no future benefit derives from payments made to former
employees, thus any unexpensed obligation with respect to those
employees should be recognized immediately. The argument in
favor of amortization is based on the concept that pension costs relate
to all plan participants on an ongoing basis, rather than to any
particular individuals. The Task Force concluded that unless an
estimate of future plant closings was already included in the turnover assumption used in calculating annual expense provisions, the
present value of vested benefits for all active employees terminated
by the closing that have not yet been charged to expense should be
expensed immediately.

A secondary issue is whether costs related to employees who
retired prior to the plant closing should be accounted for differently
than those forced to terminate as a result of the event. The rationale
for differing treatment is that the costs related to such retirees are not
changed by the closing, so there is no reason to modify the accounting treatment of those costs.

These issues are complicated by the fact that a plant closing may result in the termination of a sufficient number of employees for the IRS to consider the plan either partially or fully terminated. If the plan is fully terminated, ERISA determines the employer's obligation and current accounting literature (FASB Interpretation No. 3) deals with the accounting treatment, requiring the excess of any contingent employer liability over prior accruals to be recorded. But the situation with respect to a partial termination is not quite so clear. The PBGC has not yet issued regulations regarding partial terminations, and related accounting treatment is not well defined.

Once a liability is recorded there are also questions as to how the liability should be eliminated in future accounting periods. This issue is also relevant in respect to business combinations.

Foreign Plans

The Accounting Principles Board recognized the importance of accounting for the costs of foreign pension plans by requiring the provisions of Opinion No. 8 to be applied to cost incurred outside the United States under plans that are reasonably similar to those contemplated by the Opinion.[30]

The FASB, however, recognized the practical limitations of applying U.S. accounting principles to foreign plans, and the Board requires the provisions of Statement No. 36 to be applied to foreign plans only to the extent the information is available.

There are many practical problems. As discussed in Chapter Two, plan design and funding practices, actuarial techniques, and accounting procedures are subject to the prevailing laws and practices of the country in which they are established. Since an employer operating in several foreign locations usually will maintain separate plans in each location, actuarially determined amounts related to foreign plans will frequently be calculated on very different bases.[31]

Strict application of uniform accounting principles to all foreign plans would require significant additional calculations,[32] with an estimated incremental cost of 20% to 50%.[33] It has been argued that such additional cost to the sponsor outweighs the benefit of providing the information to financial statement users.[34] In some cases, the data necessary to perform the calculations may not even be available, making the calculations impossible at any cost.

Termination Indemnities

The issue surrounding reporting financial information on foreign plans in compliance with U.S. accounting principles extends beyond pension benefits. As discussed in Chapter Two, in many foreign countries employers are required by law to provide other benefits, such as termination indemnities.

Since there are no specific U.S. accounting guidelines for termination indemnities, it is not surprising to find a diversity of accounting practices among U.S. multinational companies. An issues paper on this topic prepared by the American Institute of Certified Public Accountants has been forwarded to the Financial Accounting Standards Board.

The appropriate accounting as described in the issues paper generally depends on the probability that the termination indemnity will be paid. The issues paper adopts the accounting principles for accrual of loss contingencies.[35] Thus, if it is probable that a liability has been incurred at the financial statement date and the amount can be reasonably estimated, the cost should be accrued. If either of those conditions is not met, but there is reasonable possibility that a liability has been incurred, the contingency for termination indemnities should simply be disclosed. Such disclosure should indicate the nature of the indemnity and provide an estimate of amount or indicate that an estimate cannot be made.

If an accrual is to be recorded, the issues paper suggests that the amount of the accrual should, if practicable, be determined in accordance with what is called the "actuarial basis." When it is not practicable to make the necessary assumptions (e.g., for salary increases, investment return, and employee turnover) as required for the "actuarial basis," the amount of the accrual should be determined on the "termination basis." These assumptions for the "actuarial basis" are similar to those presently required for accounting for pension costs; so it would appear that under many circumstances, the estimates could be made using the "actuarial basis."

Other Post-Retirement Benefits

Chapter Two discusses the nature and characteristics of the two most common post-retirement benefits other than pensions—health and death benefits. These benefits can take many forms. For death benefits, for example, some companies provide only a nominal flat dollar amount of benefit, such as $5,000, while others provide a benefit based on the retiree's salary immediately prior to retirement.

There are currently no pronouncements dealing directly with the accounting for post-retirement benefits provided outside a pension plan. The costs are usually accounted for:

- On a pay-as-you-go basis. Expense is charged at the time the benefits are paid.

- On a terminal funding basis. At the time an employee terminates his service, an amount is charged to expense equivalent to that needed to fund the expected future benefits.

It appears that relatively few companies charge the costs to expense over the employees' working lives. As noted in Chapter Three, both the pay-as-you-go and terminal funding methods are unacceptable when accounting for pension costs. With regard to recognition of an accounting liability for an obligation for such costs, it would be highly unusual for advance recognition. The following discussion is set forth in terms of expense recognition, but similar arguments would also be relevant for liability recognition if the accounting rules for pension obligations are modified.

Arguments in favor of accruing costs of other post-retirement benefits over employees' working lives include:

- Post-retirement health and death benefits are conceptually identical to pensions in that they provide financial benefits to employees (and their beneficiaries) who no longer provide services to the employer. The accounting treatment should therefore be the same.

- If these benefits were provided under a pension plan, the costs would be accounted for in the same manner as pension costs. There should not be a different result if the benefits are provided outside a pension plan.

- Rising costs and the existence of more such plans mean that the costs for other post-retirement benefits will become more significant in the future. In light of their growth it is becoming increasingly important that these costs be accrued over the working lives of the employees.

- The pay-as-you-go and terminal funding methods are unsound means of accounting for the costs, and they should be disregarded in favor of accrual-based accounting.

Arguments against accruing costs of other post-retirement benefits over employees' working lives include:

- There are important differences between the nature of pensions and other post-retirement benefits and therefore the accounting treatment should not be the same. In the case of other post-retirement benefits:

  - • There is often less predictability as to the timing and amount of benefit payments;
  - • There are no minimum or maximum funding requirements;
  - • There are generally no vesting provisions; and
  - • The benefits are not covered under ERISA to the same extent as pensions.

- Estimating the cost of health insurance many years into the future is far more difficult than estimating the cost of pension benefits. Certain possible events are not readily predictable, such as the introduction of national health insurance, which could eliminate the need, in whole or part, for private health insurance.

- Actuarial methods to estimate costs for these benefits have not been developed. Considerable work would be needed to create appropriate methods, taking into account the unique characteristics of health benefits which differ considerably from death benefits, both of which differ from pensions.

- There are a variety of approaches used to supplement a retiree's Medicare coverage. Moreover, post-retirement death benefits can take many forms and there are a variety of financing arrangements used to provide these benefits. (See Chapter Two for more information on post-retirement health and death benefits and the financing arrangements.)

- The costs of other post-retirement benefits are far less significant than pension costs. No real distortions result if pay-as-you-go expensing is used. The administrative costs to calculate other post-retirement benefit costs on an accrual basis would far outweigh the benefits to plan sponsors and users of financial statements.

NOTES

1. A. F. Ehrbar, "Those Pension Plans Are Even Weaker Than You Think," *Fortune*, XCVI, (November 1977), p. 105.

2. Deborah Rankin, "Worrying About the Pension Gap," *New York Times*, CXXX, Sec. 12, (January 8, 1979), p. 64, and
   William D. Hall and David L. Lansittel, *A New Look at Accounting for Pension Costs*, (Homewood, IL: Richard D. Irwin, Inc., 1977), p. 2.

3. A. J. C. Smith, "Unfunded Pension Liabilities: An Exaggerated Problem," *Dun's Review*, III, (February 1978), p. 85.

4. Mary Greenbaum, "The Market Has Spotted Those Pension Problems," *Fortune*, 102, (December 1, 1980), p. 143.

5. Steven Hemmerick, "IF Expands Into Corporate Area," *Pensions & Investments*, 8, (November 10, 1980), p. 35.

6. Harold M. Williams, speech given at New York State Society of Certified Public Accountants' Foundation for Accounting Education, November 3, 1980.

7. Paul A. Gerwitz and Robert C. Philips, "Unfunded Pension Liabilities . . . The New Myth," *Financial Executive*, (August, 1978), pp. 18–19, and
   William M. Mercer, Incorporated, *Living With Unfunded Pension Liabilities*, (New York, 1976), p. 2.

8. "Article Ignores Key Facts of Pension Systems" (editorial), *Pensions and Investments* (January 2, 1978), p. 16.

9. Financial Accounting Standards Board, *Statement of Financial Accounting Concepts No. 3, Elements of Financial Statements of Business Enterprises*, (Stamford, CT: FASB, December 1980), paragraph 28, p. 12.

10. Employee Retirement Security Act of 1974, *U.S. Code*, Vol. 29, Section 403(c)(1).

11. *Ibid.*, Section 4062(b)(1).

12. *Ibid.*, Section 4044(d).

13. Financial Accounting Standards Board, *Elements of Financial Statements of Business Enterprises, Exposure Draft (revised)* (Stamford, CT: FASB, December 28, 1979), paragraph 19.

14. FASB, *Statements of Financial Accounting Concepts, Statement of Financial Accounting Concepts No. 3*, paragraph 20, pp. 9–10.

15. *Ibid.*, paragraph 119, p. 55.

16. The term "fair value" is defined in FASB Statement No. 35 as—"the amount that the plan could reasonably expect to receive for it in a current sale between a willing buyer and a willing seller, that is, other than in a forced or liquidation sale."

17. Hall and Landsittel, p. 75.

18. The five acceptable actuarial cost methods are Accrued Benefit (Unit Credit), Entry Age Normal, Individual Level Premium, Aggregate and Attained Age Normal. For a description of these methods, see Chapter Three.

19. Financial Accounting Standards Board, *Conceptual Framework for Financial Accounting and Reporting: Elements of Financial Statements and Their Measurements*, (Stamford, CT: FASB, December 2, 1976), paragraph 34.

20. *Ibid.,* paragraphs 38–39.

21. *Ibid.,* paragraphs 41 and 51.

22. *Ibid.,* paragraph 74.

23. Financial Accounting Standards Board, *Statement of Financial Accounting Concepts No. 1, Objectives of Financial Reporting by Business Enterprises*, (Stamford, CT: FASB, November 1979), paragraph 34.

24. Robert S. Kemp, Robert C. Earnest and Stephen E. Celec, *An Examination of the Relevance of APB No. 8 in Reporting Unfunded Pension Liabilities*, (Tallahassee, FL: Florida State University, August 1979), (see FASB comment letter no. 99 file reference 1032–022).

25. Roy A. Schotland, "Fuller Disclosure is Needed of Obligations on the Balance Sheet," *Pensions and Investments*, 7, (November 19, 1979) p. 42.

26. American Telephone and Telegraph Company, comment letter to FASB, file reference 1024-019P, letter no. 74A, (November 2, 1979).

27. Jack L. Smith, "Needed: Improved Pension Accounting and Reporting," *Management Accounting*, 59, (May 1978), pp. 43–46. Abbott Laboratories, comment letter to FASB, file reference 1032-022, letter no. 215, (October 12, 1979).

28. As one example, a study on accounting for pension costs conducted by a group formed jointly by the AICPA and similar accounting bodies in Canada and the United Kingdom recommends disclosure of the following accounting information in the financial statements of employers, Accountant's International Study Group, *Accounting for Pension Costs: Current Practices in Canada, the United Kingdom, and the United States* (New York: Newport Press, 1977) paragraph 51:

    1. A summary of the type of pension plan(s) in force, giving such information as whether the plan is fully insured, whether the plan is defined benefit or defined contribution, a statement of the basis on which benefits are to be paid (e.g., final-year or final-career average earnings), and the category of employees covered. Any guarantee given to maintain the solvency of the plan should also be disclosed.
    2. Disclosure of the accounting and funding policies adopted for pension costs.
    3. Disclosure of the actuarial cost method and the method of asset valuation which was used as a basis for arriving at the amount of pension cost and liability.
    4. Disclosure of the charge against income for pension costs for the period, distinguishing between the part that should be attributable to (a) current service pension costs, and (b) prior service costs including interest thereon; and separate disclosure of adjustments arising from actuarial revaluations.
    5. Disclosure of any significant pension matters affecting comparability with the previous period, including, for example, where there has been a change in the actuarial cost method or asset valuation method, disclosure of the financial effect of the change and of the reason for making the change.
    6. Except to the extent that it is recognized in the balance sheet, disclosure of the

legal liability, if any, of the employer that would result from termination of the plan, where termination is imminent.

7. Disclosure of any significant holding by the fund of the employer's shares, debentures or loan capital, or of any asset of the fund which represents a significant proportion of its total assets.

29. *Connolly v. PBGC* (CA-9 rev'g DC Cal) 581 F2d 729.

30. American Institute of Certified Public Accountants, *Accounting Principles Board Opinion No. 8: Accounting for the Cost of Pension Plans* (New York: AICPA, November 1966), paragraph 8, pp. 2–3.

31. An exception would be where an employer maintains a special plan exclusively for U.S. expatriates or third country nationals. These plans are usually, but not always, maintained outside the U.S.

32. W.R. Grace & Co., comment letter to FASB, file reference 1032-022, no. 178, (September 26, 1979).

33. Texas Instruments Incorporated, comment letter to FASB, file reference 1032-022, no. 203, (September 28, 1979).

34. See comment letters to FASB, file reference 1032-022P, Armstrong Cork Company, letter no. 39, (September 17, 1979). Royal Dutch/Shell Group of Companies, letter no. 41, (September 14, 1979). Johnson & Higgins, letter no. 63, (September 21, 1979). 3M Company, letter no. 90, (September 19, 1979). Dresser Industries, letter no. 167, (September 21, 1979). Singer Company, letter no. 199, (September 27, 1979).

35. It adopts the principles of *Statement of Financial Accounting Standards No. 5, Accounting for Contingencies* (March 1975) of the Financial Accounting Standards Board.

Six

Survey and Interview Findings

In our preliminary research we identified the issues and alternatives affecting accounting for pension costs and other post-retirement benefits (see Chapter Five). The resulting data was then used to develop a comprehensive questionnaire, which served as the basis of our mail survey and personal interviews.

The objective of the survey and interviews was to obtain the views of corporate executives and others who are involved with the preparation or use of financial statements and actuarial information. In this regard, the response to both the mail survey and interviews indicated great familiarity with the issues.

This chapter describes the methodology used and reports the findings. The material is organized into the following sections:

- *Methodology.* Development and testing of the questionnaire; selection of respondents; and survey and interview procedures.

- *Analysis of Overall Response.*

- *Findings on Key Issues.* The responses to key questions are reported, including our observations. The key issues are categorized as follows:

    - • User Data—Use of financial data on pension costs by financial analysts, creditors, and others.
    - • Basic issues (e.g., perception of a plan as an ongoing or terminating entity).

- • Pension cost recognition (e.g., recording an obligation).
- • Disclosure.
- • Special issues (e.g., plant closings, business combinations, treatment of foreign plans, etc.).
- • Other post-retirement benefits.

- *Appendix.* The questionnaire with tabulated results for the mail survey and interviews.

METHODOLOGY

Development and Testing of the Questionnaire

A single, comprehensive questionnaire was developed for use in the mail survey and interviews. The organization of the questionnaire reflects a sensitivity to the various types of respondents participating in the study (i.e., company executives, users of financial statements, and other respondents) and their different needs in using pension cost information. Sections I–III of the questionnaire were designed to obtain information about the respondents; Sections IV–VIII focused on the respondents' views about the issues and alternatives.

Generally, the questions in Sections IV–VIII are multiple choice; the respondents were asked to identify the degree to which they agreed or disagreed with a given statement. For certain questions, the respondents were asked to rank and weight given alternatives.

The questionnaire was reviewed by the Financial Executives Research Foundation Project Advisory Committee, the Coopers & Lybrand research team, and other Partners of our Firm. Four test interviews were conducted and fifty test questionnaires were mailed to selected respondents. As a result of the testing, the questionnaire was modified slightly for use in the mail survey and interviews.

Selection of Respondents for the Mail Survey and Interviews

Determination of Universe. The universe was basically developed from the:

- AICPA Directory of Members.

- American Academy of Actuaries Directory of Members.

- Finance Directory of Investment Bankers and Brokers.

- Financial Executives Institute Membership List.

- Fortune 1,000 List of Industrial Companies.

From the universe, a random, yet balanced sample was selected using these criteria to identify types of respondents:

- Users of financial statements (e.g., financial analysts, commercial banks).

- Plan sponsors (company executives).

- Other respondents (e.g., consulting actuaries and independent public accountants).

The respondents were further classified by:

- Industry group—the nature of each respondent's business was identified, using the Standard Industrial Classification system.

- Size—the relative size of each respondent's business was identified by the total sales or revenues and the number of employees.

Mail Survey Sample.   2,561 respondents were identified for the mail survey—50 respondents were then selected from the sample to test the questionnaire.

Interview Sample.   Initially, 55 respondents were selected as candidates for personal interviews. (Selection of a larger number of candidates allowed for alternate choices if an interview was refused.)

From this group, 37 respondents were selected as participants for the personal interviews and 4 of the 37 respondents were identified for test interviews.

Mail Survey and Interview Procedures

Mail Survey.   The questionnaire was mailed to each respondent with a cover letter from the Financial Executives Research Foundation explaining the purpose and importance of the survey. The respondents were asked to complete the questionnaire and mail it directly to Coopers & Lybrand.

Interview Procedures.   An introductory letter including Sections I and II or I and III of the questionnaire was mailed to each selected respondent. Those who wished to participate were asked to complete Sections I and II or I and III and return them to Coopers & Lybrand along with the name(s) of the individual(s) who would participate in the interview. In many instances, a team of individuals (including financial, accounting, and human resources executives) from a company participated in the interview.

The in-depth interviews were usually conducted at the respondent's offices by two Coopers & Lybrand Partners—one with an accounting background and another with extensive experience in employee benefits. During the interviews, which generally lasted two to four hours, Sections IV–VIII of the questionnaire were reviewed and completed. Key issues were discussed in detail, and respondents' comments were solicited.

ANALYSIS OF OVERALL RESPONSE

Total Response

Mail Survey.   Of the 2,511 questionnaires mailed to selected respondents, 516 questionnaires were returned. However, 118 of the returned questionnaires were not usable in the compilation of results for a variety of factors (e.g., 21 of the questionnaires were returned unanswered because the respondents did not maintain a defined benefit pension plan). The results from 398 questionnaires were used in the compilation, representing a response rate of 16%.

Interviews.   Of the 37 respondents who were contacted to participate in the interviews, 30 were actually interviewed, representing a response rate of 81%.

Total Study.   Of the 2,548 prospective respondents contacted for either the mail survey or personal interviews, 428 usable responses were received, representing a total response rate of 17%.

Response Analysis

Response from the mail survey and the interviews were combined. The exhibit on page 93 shows the make-up of the total group of respondents by types.

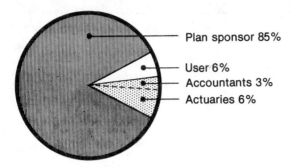

The respondents were also classified by industry. The distribution of respondents among industrial groups is presented on page 94.

Further classification of the respondents by size resulted in the distribution shown on the top of page 95.

An analysis of the respondent group who completed Section II of the questionnaire (plan sponsors) indicates how frequently certain benefits are provided. This is also shown on page 95.

FINDINGS ON KEY ISSUES

Reporting Format

This section reports in detail the responses to key issues. In each instance, the issue is identified and presentation of the findings generally includes:

- The survey question.

- A statistical report of the responses from the mail survey and interviews.

- Our observations which include further analysis of the statistical

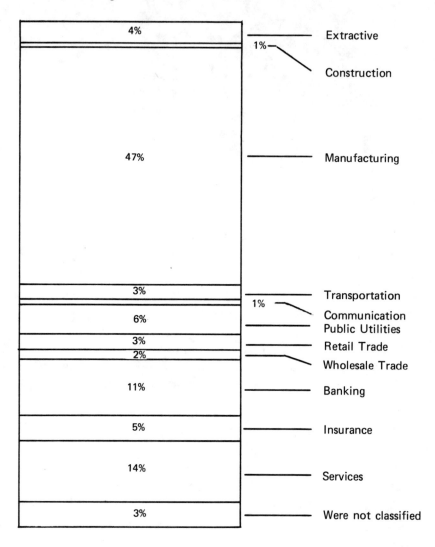

responses as well as some analysis of comments received during the personal interviews.

For a number of the key issues, supplementary information is provided in the form of additional analysis correlating the statistical responses to two or more questions. When included, the correlative data immediately precedes our observations.

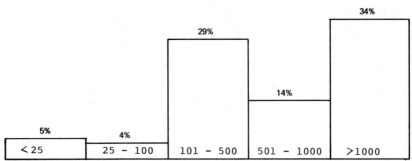

34%

29%

14%

5%

4%

| < 25 | 25 - 100 | 101 - 500 | 501 - 1000 | >1000 |

in millions of US$ sales

(14% did not supply financial data.)

Based on response from 366 respondents.

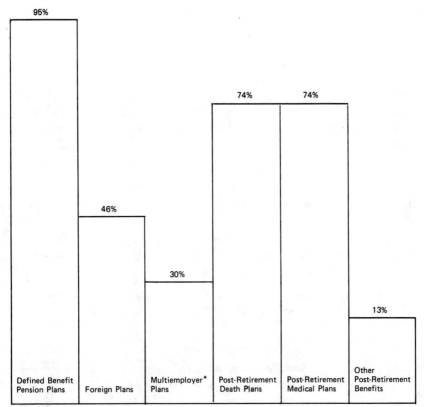

95%

74%   74%

46%

30%

13%

Defined Benefit Pension Plans | Foreign Plans | Multiemployer* Plans | Post-Retirement Death Plans | Post-Retirement Medical Plans | Other Post-Retirement Benefits

*Respondent makes contributions to a multiemployer plan.

USER DATA—USE OF FINANCIAL DATA ON PENSION COSTS BY FINANCIAL ANALYSTS, CREDITORS, AND OTHERS

Uses of Pension Information

Question 3.02. For what major purpose are your analyses of pension accounting information used?

Credit decisions	31%
Investment decisions	44%
Economic research	0%
Investment banking	0%
Other	13%
Inadequate response*	12%

*Wherever it appears, the inadequate response indicates all respondents who did not know, did not respond, or responded more than once to the question.

Observations: Reported pension cost data is most often used for credit or investment decisions. A number of interview respondents indicated that for some credit analyses pension costs are imputed as part of the fixed costs of a company's operations. For example, all or a portion of unfunded prior service costs may be treated as debt. This is generally done when there is a concern about a company's ability to meet its obligations.

Effect of Pension Information on Analyses and Decisions

Question 3.05. To what extent has pension accounting data affected your analyses and decisions regarding specific companies? (Please rank in terms of frequency with "1" being the most frequent.)

NOTE: The response given below represents the frequency that the option was either selected or ranked "1."

No effect	25%
Confirmed other data	35%
Tempered conclusions which otherwise would have been reached	14%
Substantially altered conclusions	4%

Reversed conclusions	0%
Inadequate response	22%

Observations: Financial information about reported pension cost data in a sponsoring employer's financial statements is not likely to substantially alter or reverse user conclusions. Interview respondents generally indicated that the information is not very useful except as a starting point; for instance, it is helpful when analyzing a labor-intensive company that may be experiencing financial difficulties.

The remaining groups of key issues relate to all survey respondents, not just users of financial statements.

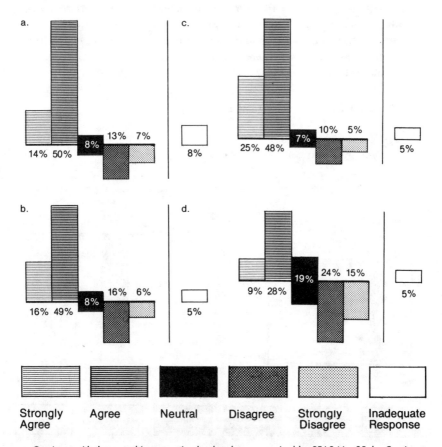

a. Consistent with those used in accounting by the plan, as required by SFAS No. 35. b. Consistent with those used for funding purposes. c. Consistently applied with respect to each of the company's defined benefit plans. d. Consistent with those used by other employers maintaining defined benefit plans.

BASIC ISSUES

Consistency in Financial Reporting

Question 4.01. The methods and techniques used in accounting for pension costs by the sponsoring employer should generally be:

Observations: Most respondents were sensitive to the unique characteristics of individual plans and their sponsors. Thus, only 39% of the respondents felt that the methods and techniques used in accounting for pension costs should be consistent with those used by other employers who maintain defined benefit pension plans.

A significant number of interview respondents indicated that the methods and techniques should not be consistent with respect to each defined benefit plan because every plan and sponsor is unique. Others indicated that the methods and techniques could be consistent with those used by other employers only if the employers were maintaining the same defined benefit plan.

Perception of the Plan as an Ongoing or Terminating Entity

Question 4.02. In accounting for pension costs by the sponsoring employer, it should generally be assumed that the plan is:

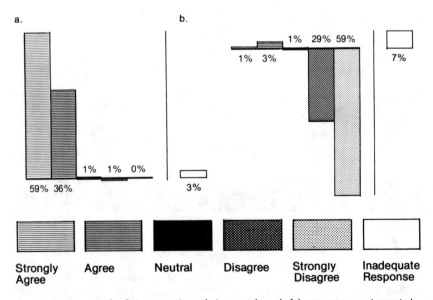

a. An ongoing entity. b. Going to terminate during or at the end of the current accounting period.

Observations: Nearly all the respondents (95%) agreed that the plan should be assumed to be an ongoing entity for accounting purposes; approximately 4% indicated a preference for assuming the plan is a terminating entity. Many interview respondents supported this result by stating that the plan should be considered ongoing so long as the company is healthy, viable, and not threatened, because the health of the private pension plan follows the health of the plan sponsor.

Relative Importance of Certain Financial Reporting Items in Assessing a Sponsoring Employer's Pension Costs

In Question 4.03 the respondents were asked to indicate the importance of certain items, for financial reporting purposes, in assessing a sponsoring employer's pension costs. The respondents clearly identified pension expense as the most important aspect of assessing a sponsoring employer's pension costs. The next most important items were identified as "some measure of an obligation and the value of plan assets," "the amount actually funded for the period," and "the actuarial cost method and assumptions used for expense purposes."

For a listing of the financial reporting items considered and the survey response, see the Appendix.

PENSION COST RECOGNITION

Actuarial Considerations in Expense Measurement

Question 5.04. With respect to the actuarial cost method used to calculate expense see graphs next page:

Observations: A majority of the respondents (55%) indicated a preference for retaining the cost methods in APB Opinion No. 8, while 20% indicated a need to change. As to permitting additional alternatives, 18% felt that more alternatives should be permitted but 22% indicated that fewer alternatives should be allowed.

Most respondents (over 73%) disagreed with an alternative that would require all sponsors to determine expense, using the same actuarial method. Only 15% of the respondents agreed with this alternative. In addition, numerous interview respondents observed that a choice of an actuarial cost method should be allowed based on the characteristics of the sponsor's plan and the sponsor's financial forecast. They noted that companies are allowed to have a choice among acceptable methods in other areas such as depreciation and valuing inventories.

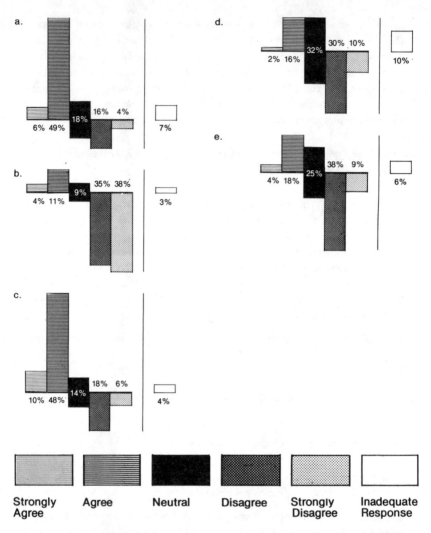

a. Current APB Opinion No. 8 requirements should be retained. b. One actuarial cost method should be prescribed. c. The same actuarial cost method used by the sponsoring employers in pension plan funding calculations should be required. d. Additional alternatives to those in APB opinion No. 8 should be permitted. e. Fewer alternatives to those in APB Opinion No. 8 should be permitted.

The option with the greatest positive response was (c)—use the same actuarial cost method used by the sponsoring employer in pension plan funding calculation—58% agreed; 24% disagreed; 14% were neutral.

In Question 5.06 we asked a similar question on actuarial assumptions, i.e., whether the current flexibility permitted in APB Opinion No. 8 regarding the selection of actuarial assumptions should be retained.

INDUSTRY   ACTUAL RESPONSE

	Strongly Agree	Agree	Neutral	Dis-agree	Strongly Disagree	Inadequate Response	Total Respon-dents
Manufacturing	5	39	20	74	60	3	201
Public utilities	0	8	1	13	5	0	27
Banking & finance	5	14	2	16	11	1	49
Insurance	2	2	3	11	2	2	22
Services	5	17	6	8	14	2	52
							351

(11 respondents were not classified and 66 respondents represented industry groups that were not significantly represented by the survey respondent group)

Nearly three-fourths of the respondents (72%) agreed with the statement and only 16% disagreed. There was also significant agreement on requiring the sponsoring employer to use the same actuarial assumptions that were used for funding purposes to calculate expense (58% agreed; 25% disagreed).

The response to two options that would limit the choice in actuarial assumptions (one option would prescribe specific quantitative amounts while the second option would prescribe specific types of actuarial assumptions) was decidedly negative—76% disagreed with specifying quantitative amounts (12% agreed); 55% disagreed with specifying specific types (31% agreed).

RECORDING AN OBLIGATION

Recording a Measure of the Plan's Obligation for Benefits As a Liability on the Sponsoring Employer's Balance Sheet

Question 5.10. Some measure of the obligation should be recorded as a liability in the sponsoring employer's balance sheet.

Strongly Agree	5%
Agree	24%
Neutral	8%
Disagree	35%
Strongly Disagree	26%
Inadequate Response	2%

Additional Analyses

A.   The response to the question of recording an obligation was broken down by respondent type, and is shown on page 101.

B.   The response by plan sponsors to the question of recording an obligation was broken down by industry as follows:

Observations: A majority of the respondents (61%) disagreed with the statement that some measure of a pension obligation should be recorded as an accounting liability. 29% indicated that a liability should be recorded.

A breakdown of respondents by "user," "plan sponsor," and "other" does not result in a significant variance in the response pattern. However, when the "other respondent" group is broken down into its two major components, actuaries and accountants, the response pattern

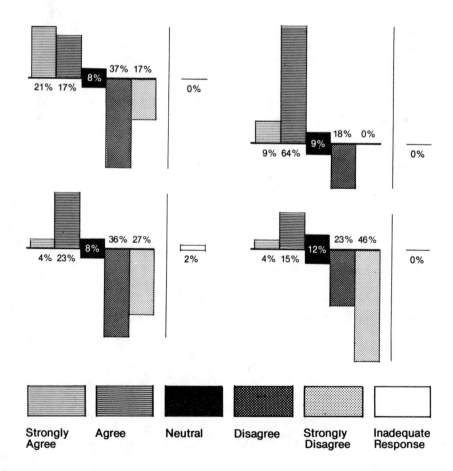

| Strongly Agree | Agree | Neutral | Disagree | Strongly Disagree | Inadequate Response |

changes considerably. The response which is attributable to the actuaries is clearly negative (69% disagreed) while the independant accountants' response was strongly positive (73% agreed).

All but three of the industry groups responded to the question negatively. For certain groups the response was very negative (e.g., 134 of the respondents in the manufacturing industry disagreed and only 44 agreed) whereas in other groups nearly as many respondents agreed as disagreed. For example, in the services group 22 agreed and 22 disagreed.

Of those respondents who indicated that some measure of a liability should be recorded, most favored using either vested benefits (43%) or accumulated benefits (SFAS No. 35) (46%) as the measure of the obligation. Only 7% favored PBGC guaranteed benefits.

DISCLOSURE

FASB Exposure Draft and SFAS No. 36 Requirements for Disclosure of Pension Information

Question 6.02. As an interim measure pending completion of its comprehensive project on "Accounting by Employers for Pensions," the FASB issued an Exposure Draft, "Disclosure of Pension and Other Post-Retirement Benefit Information," which would require additional pension cost disclosures. In its final statement, SFAS 36, the FASB decided that—(1) required disclosure of significant actuarial assumptions will be limited to the assumed interest rate, (2) separate disclosure of information related to grouping of over- and under-funded plans will not be required, and (3) annual benefit valuations for plans with more than 100 participants will not be required. Please indicate your view by checking the appropriate box. (See chart next page.)

Observations: In response to several items of disclosure required by SFAS No. 36 or the preceding exposure draft, most respondents (70%) agreed with disclosure of the actuarial present value of vested benefits. As to the other items, 68% agreed with disclosure of the fair market value of the plan's net assets available for benefits; 57% agreed with disclosure of a description of significant actuarial assumptions and asset valuation methods; 55% agreed with disclosure of the assumed rate of return; and 52% agreed with disclosure of the actuarial present value of accumulated benefits.

	Agree Strongly that Disclosure Should be Required	Agree that Disclosure Should be Required	Neutral	Agree that Disclosure Should Not be Required	Agree Strongly that Disclosure Should Not be Required	Inadequate Response
(a) The actuarial present value of accumulated benefits.	14%	38%	20%	21%	5%	2%
(b) The actuarial present value of vested benefits.	18%	52%	14%	11%	3%	2%
(c) The fair market value of the plan's net assets available for benefits.	18%	50%	14%	13%	3%	2%
(d) A description of significant actuarial assumptions and as set valuation methods used to determine (a), (b), and (c) above.	14%	43%	18%	19%	4%	2%
(e) The assumed rate of return used to determine (a) and (b).	12%	43%	20%	18%	4%	3%
(f) For employers with more than one ongoing plan, plans should be grouped as to those that have: (1) an actuarial present value of accumulated plan benefits in excess of net as- sets, and (2) net assets avail- able for benefits in excess of the actuarial present value of plan benefits.	5%	26%	27%	25%	10%	7%

A number of interview respondents expressed concern that if too much information is disclosed, confusion could result. For example, undue alarm could result from focusing on incorrect relationships such as pension expense as a percentage of total revenues. Many respondents also showed concern about placing too much importance on pension cost information relative to other financial statement data. As indicated earlier in our observations to Question 4.03, respondents again confirmed that pension expense is the most important aspect of assessing a plan sponsor's pension cost data.

Selection of the Appropriate Measure of the Obligation Where One Measure is Required for Disclosure Purposes

Question 6.06.   If a single measure of the obligation is required to be disclosed, it should be based on (check one):

Observations: Most of the respondents agreed (50%) that if one single measure of the obligation is required to be disclosed, it should be vested benefits. Of the remaining options, 36% of the respondents agreed that accumulated benefits, calculated in accordance with SFAS No. 35, is the appropriate measure; while less than 12% agreed that PBGC guaranteed benefits or unfunded past service costs, as historically required by the Securities and Exchange Commission, is the appropriate measure.

SPECIAL ISSUES

Plant Closings

Question 7.03.   Rather than recognizing an actuarial gain or loss, any obligation for unfunded vested benefits related to participants in the plant should be charged to income.

Strongly Agree	1%
Agree	23%
Neutral	17%
Disagree	35%
Strongly Disagree	10%
Inadequate Response	14%

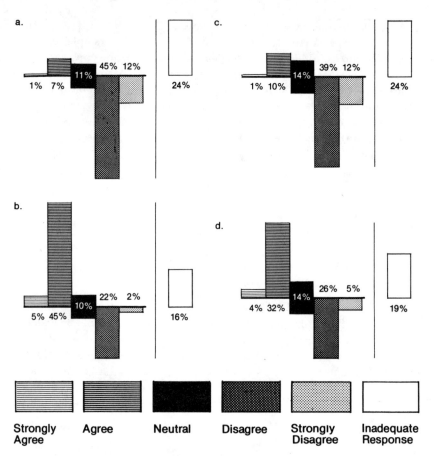

a. PBGC guaranteed benefits. b. Vested benefits. c. Unfunded past service costs, historically required by the SEC. d. Accumulated benefits (SFAS No. 35).

Observations: Nearly half (45%) of the respondents disagreed with the statement that an obligation for unfunded vested benefits arising as a result of a plant closing should be charged immediately to income. About one-fourth (24%) of the respondents agreed with the statement. A relatively large number of respondents (14%) did not know or did not give an answer.

Numerous interview respondents observed that more guidance is needed in accounting for plant closings. Many reported that more direction is needed in accounting for work force reductions in general, whether or not a plant closing occurs. Others stated concern about the appropriate measure of an accounting liability in the event of a plant closing.

Business Combinations

Question 7.06. The accounting treatment required by APB Opinion No. 16 should be unchanged.

Strongly Agree	Negligible
Agree	30%
Neutral	24%
Disagree	23%
Strongly Disagree	4%
Inadequate Response	19%

Observations: A number of interview respondents expressed concern about whether a liability should be recorded at all. APB Opinion No. 16 requires, in an acquisition accounted for under the purchase method, that a liability should be recorded in the amount of the greater of: (1) accrued pension cost computed in conformity with the accounting policies of the acquiring company or, (2) the unfunded vested benefits. Others were more concerned about the measure of any liability. Again, a relatively large number of respondents (19%) did not know or did not give an answer.

Multiemployer Plans

Question 7.10. Employer accounting for multiemployer defined benefit plans should be subject to the same accounting rules as single employer defined benefit plans.

	Total Response	Only Respondents that Contribute to Multiemployer Plans
Strongly Agree	5%	0%
Agree	38%	30%
Neutral	14%	8%
Disagree	12%	24%
Strongly Disagree	9%	23%
Inadequate Response	22%	15%

Observations: Over one-third of the respondents did not know enough about the issue to respond, were neutral, or simply did not respond. As noted earlier, 70% of the plan sponsors do not make contributions to a multiemployer plan. It is also noted that the response from companies that contribute to multiemployer plans is considerably more negative. A number of interview respondents indicated a concern about the availability of good data and the unknown impact of the Multiemployer Pension Plan Amendments Act of 1980.

Foreign Plans

Question 7.11. Employer accounting for costs related to foreign defined benefit plans should be subject to the same accounting rules as domestic plans.

	Total Response	Only Respondents with Foreign Plans
Strongly Agree	3%	4%
Agree	36%	38%
Neutral	14%	11%
Disagree	19%	30%
Strongly Disagree	6%	12%
Inadequate Response	22%	5%

Observations: In general, more respondents agreed (rather than disagreed) that employer accounting for costs related to foreign defined benefit plans should be subject to the same accounting rules as domestic plans. However, when examining the response from respondents who maintain foreign plans, the number of respondents who disagreed increases considerably. In this regard, many interview respondents expressed a concern about availability of information, the cost to produce required information and the significance of the information.

OTHER POST-RETIREMENT BENEFITS

Data on the Other Post-Retirement Benefits Provided by the Survey Respondents

Question 2.13. What post-retirement benefits does your company provide?

Health Insurance	74%
Life Insurance	74%
Other	13%

(This is based on responses from 366 respondents.)

Observations: Many companies are providing post-retirement health and death benefits for retirees. Nearly three-fourths of the respondents to this survey question provide these benefits.

Question 2.14. How do you account for the expense associated with these other post-retirement benefits?

	Health	Death	Other*
(a) Pay-as-you-go (i.e., amount paid is expensed).	96%	82%	54%
(b) Expense is accrued over employees' working lives.	1%	10%	31%
(c) Terminal basis (i.e., recording expense upon the retirement of the employee).	2%	3%	6%
(d) Other method	1%	3%	4%
Inadequate response	0%	2%	5%

*Other refers to post-retirement benefits other than pensions, health, or death benefits. The respondents did not identify specific benefits in this category.

Observations: Nearly all of the respondents (96% for health benefits and 82% for death benefits) account for the expense on a "pay-as-you-go" basis.

Question 2.17. Estimate the annual accounting expense and annual amount of benefit payments (expressed as a percent of the payroll for active employees covered by all pension plans) for providing post-retirement benefits:

Annual Expenditure Expressed as Percent of Payroll	Health Insurance		Life Insurance	
	Expense	Payments	Expense	Payments
1% or Less	39%	40%	43%	41%
1% to 3%	8%	6%	5%	5%
3% to 6%	4%	5%	1%	2%
Over 6%	1%	1%	0%	0%
Inadequate Response	48%	48%	51%	52%

(Percentages based on 273 respondents who provide post-retirement health insurance and 273 respondents who provide post-retirement life insurance.)

Observations: Nearly all respondents have expense of less than 1% of payroll for post-retirement health and death benefits. The response shows that the expense and benefit payments are generally the same. This provides further support to the results for Question 2.14 that the costs for these benefits are generally expensed on a "pay-as-you-go" basis.

We asked a similar question concerning pension expense and pension benefit payments in Question 2.06. The greatest number of respondents reported pension expense of 5% to 10% of payroll. The difference between reported pension expense and reported expense for other post-retirement benefits is significant. However, it is not really possible

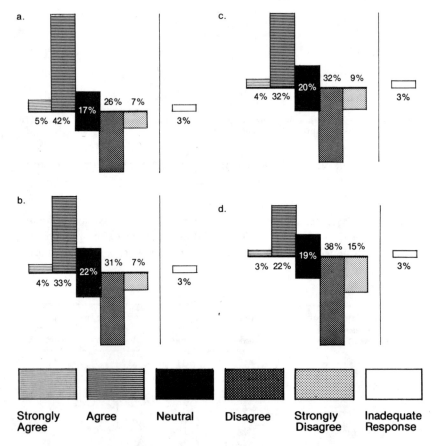

a. The existence of other post-retirement benefits. b. The accounting policy for those benefits. c. The cost of the benefits in determining net income for the period. d. Some measure on a present value basis of the obligation for these benefits, along with the actuarial methods and assumptions used.

to accurately compare pension expense with expense for other post-retirement benefits since the computation methods are radically different. Pension costs are generally expensed over the working lives of the employees, whereas post-retirement benefit costs are almost always expensed on a pay-as-you-go basis. The only way of making a fair comparison would be through some form of complicated modeling. Moreover, it is difficult to assess the magnitude of other post-retirement benefits without having more information (e.g., knowledge about the benefits provided the employee group, the characteristics of the employee group, and financing arrangements).

Required Disclosure About Other Post-Retirement Benefits

Question 8.01.   Indicate your view by checking the appropriate box. Disclosure of the following should be required (as shown on page 110):

Observations: Many respondents (approximately 25%) did not answer or were neutral on the question of disclosure. In addition, the interview respondents appeared to be less knowledgeable about post-retirement benefits when compared to pension plans and thus offered fewer comments.

The survey response indicates that a greater percentage of respondents favor disclosing the existence of other post-retirement benefits (47% agreed, 33% disagreed) than the other possibilities. Many of the interview comments were similar in nature. Respondents observed that the costs are not likely to be material, methodology needs to be developed to estimate costs, and if disclosures are to be required, work needs to be done to obtain more data about existing plans.

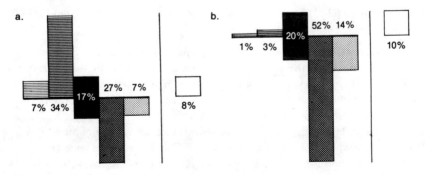

a. Pay-as-you-go. b. Terminal funding basis.

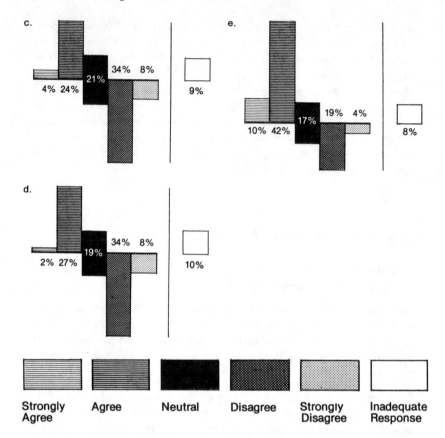

Strongly Agree | Agree | Neutral | Disagree | Strongly Disagree | Inadequate Response

c. Accrued over the working lives of the participants. d. Treated in the same manner as pension costs.
e. No one method should be required.

Determination of Expense Related to Other Post-Retirement Benefits

Question 8.02. The expense provision for those costs should be accounted for as follows:

Observations: More than half the respondents indicated that one method for accounting for the expense associated with other post-retirement benefits should not be required (52% agreed, 23% disagreed). Of the methods offered as options in Question 8.02, only (a) pay-as-you-go received an overall positive response (41% agreed, 34% disagreed). However, many respondents (about 28%) did not answer or were neutral on the question of expense. This again indicates a lack of formulated opinions concerning the treatment of other post-retirement benefits.

FINANCIAL EXECUTIVES RESEARCH FOUNDATION

QUESTIONNAIRE ON

ACCOUNTING FOR PENSION COSTS AND

OTHER POST-RETIREMENT BENEFITS

C O O P E R S   &   L Y B R A N D

A MEMBER FIRM OF

COOPERS & LYBRAND (INTERNATIONAL)

1251 AVENUE OF THE AMERICAS

NEW YORK, N.Y. 10020

July 8, 1980

We are currently conducting a study on <u>accounting for pension costs and other post-retirement benefits</u> for the Financial Executives Research Foundation -- the research arm of the Financial Executives Institute. The attached questionnaire is an important part of this effort.

The questionnaire is being sent to a sample of users and preparers of financial statements. It is also being sent to representatives of the public accounting and actuarial professions and other interested parties. The results of this survey will be made available to the Financial Accounting Standards Board for use in its deliberations on accounting for the cost of pensions and other post-retirement benefits.

The success of this project requires your assistance. We would appreciate it if you would take the time to complete the questionnaire. Our experience indicates that it will take approximately 1-1/2 hours to complete. Your completed questionnaire will be maintained in complete confidence. Responses will be reported only in tabular form, and company identities will be known only to Coopers & Lybrand. The study's results are to be included in a report to be published by the Financial Executives Research Foundation.

Please return the completed questionnaire in the enclosed self-addressed envelope by July 31, 1980. Thank you for your cooperation.

Coopers & Lybrand

INTRODUCTION

Accounting for pension costs is a complex and controversial subject involving the measurement and prediction of future events. These events include future earnings of pension fund investments, employee salaries, and patterns of employee turnover and mortality.

The applicable accounting pronouncements generally allow significant latitude in the measurement of pension costs. A variety of actuarial methods and assumptions is permitted with the selection being left to the judgment of company management and its actuaries. The question of whether present accounting practice meaningfully presents the financial impact of employer responsibilities under a pension plan is actively being discussed. A number of articles in the financial press have focused on "unfunded pension liabilities."

Recently, the Financial Accounting Standards Board issued SFAS 36 entitled "Disclosure of Pension Information." The statement, which is effective for fiscal years beginning after December 15, 1979 amends certain disclosure requirements of Accounting Principles Board Opinion No. 8 and represents an interim measure pending the completion of the FASB's comprehensive re-examination of employer accounting for pension costs. That project is in its early stages, and it is intended that it will result in an FASB statement specifying financial accounting standards. The results of this questionnaire and the other aspects of our study will be furnished to the FASB for use in connection with that project.

Note that the thrust of this questionnaire is directed at accounting by the sponsoring employer company, and generally only with respect to its funded defined benefit pension plans maintained in the United States. Accounting for the costs of defined contribution plans, foreign pension plans, and termination indemnities, and accounting for the plan as an entity,* are not covered. A separate section of this questionnaire is devoted to the employer company's accounting for post-retirement benefits other than pensions.

There are a number of broad issues that are central to accounting for pension costs, including: whether or not a pension plan "obligation" should be recorded as an accounting liability on the sponsoring company's balance sheet; whether an obligation should instead only be disclosed in the notes to the financial statements; how a pension obligation should be measured; and whether the expense provision for pensions should continue to be measured in accordance with the provisions of APB Opinion No. 8. Questions arise as to the relationship between expense measurement and measurement of an obligation, between accounting and funding requirements, and comparability among companies.

To address these and related issues, the questionnaire contains the following sections:

Section	Topic	Beginning On Page
I.	General Information	5
II.	Plan Sponsor Data	6
III.	User Data	9
IV.	Perception of the Issues	10
V.	Pension Cost Recognition	12
VI.	Disclosures Regarding Pension Costs	16
VII.	Special Issues	23
VIII.	Other Post-Retirement Benefits	25

To achieve consistency in the interpretation of terms used in this questionnaire, we have included a Glossary on page 27. It may be helpful to review the Glossary before you answer the questionnaire.

The questionnaire covers some highly complex areas of accounting for pension costs. Accordingly, certain questions may relate to matters unfamiliar to some respondents. If you are unable to answer a question, please check the "Do Not Know" (DNK) category.

If you have any questions regarding this study, please contact Mr. Harold Dankner, Coopers & Lybrand, in New York City, (212) 489-1100.

*In March 1980, the FASB issued SFAS 35 entitled "Accounting and Reporting by Defined Benefit Pension Plans."

SECTION I

General Information

Name of Company _____

Volume of Sales (in millions) _____

Name and Position of Person(s) Completing Questionnaire _____

Name

_____

Title

For purposes of this questionnaire respondents are categorized in one of three groups: (1) Company executives, (2) Users of financial accounting data, or (3) Other respondents. "Company executives" include financial and other executives involved with financial reporting, as well as human resources and other executives having involvement with their company's pension plans. "Users" include individuals who analyze and use financial accounting information for making investment, credit, or other decisions. "Other respondents" include individuals who provide advice to company management.

If you are a "company executive" how would you classify yourself?

Chief Executive Officer	0
Chief Financial Officer	86
Chief Accounting Officer	70
Financial Executive	98
Accounting Executive	60
Human Resources Executive	15
Other (please describe)	21
More Than One Answer	16
Total	366

If you are a "user" how would you classify yourself?

Commercial Banker	4
Financial Analyst	6
Investment Adviser	1
Insurance Carrier	2
Other (please describe)	10
More Than One Answer	1
Total	24

If you are an "other respondent" how would you classify yourself?

Independent Public Accountant	11
Actuary	26
Attorney	0
Other (please describe)	1
Total	38

"Company executives" should complete Sections II and IV through VIII of this questionnaire. "Users" should complete Sections III through VIII. "Other respondents" should complete Sections IV through VIII. In view of its scope, you may wish to coordinate completion of this questionnaire with other personnel in your organization.

SECTION II

Plan Sponsor Data

This Section Should Be Answered By Company Executives Only

Please indicate your response by checking the appropriate box.

2.01 Number of defined benefit pension plans sponsored by the company:

18	107	59	30	153	61	428
None	One	Two	Three	More Than Three	No Answer	Total

2.02 Approximate current value (in millions) of pension fund assets (include value of unallocated insurance contracts) for all plans noted above:

50	144	117	18	23	76	428
$10 or Less	$10 To $75	$75 To $500	$500 To $1,000	Over $1,000	No Answer	Total

2.03 Number of plan participants (as reported on Form 5500) covered by all the plans noted above _____.

30	115	59	91	21	112	428
1000 Or Less	1001-5000	5001-10,000	10,001-50,000	Over 50,000	No Answer	Total

2.04 How many years has the company maintained a defined benefit plan(s)?

9	7	15	23	303	71	428
Not Applicable	5 Or Less	6 To 10	11 To 15	Over 15 Years	No Answer	Total

2.05 For your **largest** defined benefit plan (based on number of participants covered) please indicate what actuarial method is used for financial statement (expense) and funding purposes:

	Financial Statement (Expense) Purposes	Funding Purposes
Accrued Benefit (Unit Credit)	57	60
Entry Age Normal	125	127
Individual Level Premium	0	0
Aggregate	36	36
Attained Age Normal	8	4
Frozen Initial Liability	61	64
Other (please describe.)	16	15
More Than One Answer	40	40
No Answer	85	82
Total	428	428

2.06 Estimated current pension expense, expressed as a percent of payroll for **all plans** _____ %, and estimated current pension benefit payments, expressed as a percent of payroll _____ %.

Pension Expense

23	87	173	52	93	428
3% Or Less	3% To 6%	6% To 12%	Over 12%	No Answer	Total

Pension Benefit Payments

139	110	55	12	112	428
3% Or Less	3% To 6%	6% To 12%	Over 12%	No Answer	Total

2.07 Generally, how familiar are you with the accounting requirements under APB No. 8 for the cost of pension plans?

Very familiar	150
Somewhat familiar	179
Not very familiar	29
Not at all familiar	4
No answer	66
Total	428

Multiemployer Plans

2.08 Does your company make contributions to a **multiemployer plan**?

111	251	3	63	428
Yes	No	DNK	No Answer	Total

If No, Do Not Answer Questions 2.09 to 2.11.

2.09 Is the multiemployer plan treated as a defined benefit plan or defined contribution plan for financial reporting purposes?

33	60	20	315	428
Defined Benefit Plan	Defined Contribution Plan	DNK	No Answer	Total

2.10 Is the amount to be funded for the period used as the expense for financial reporting purposes?

106	9	6	307	428
Yes	No	DNK	No Answer	Total

2.11 Does the plan administrator of the multiemployer plan make available actuarial data to enable the company to determine its share of pension expense and disclosures in accordance with APB No. 8?

31	69	16	312	428
Yes	No	DNK	No Answer	Total

Foreign Plans

2.12 Are actuarial data available on defined benefit plans of the company's **foreign** units to enable the company to determine pension expense and disclosures in accordance with APB No. 8?

118	116	31	161	2	428
Yes	No	DNK	No Answer	More Than One Answer	Total

Other Post-Retirement Benefits

2.13 What post-retirement benefits other than pension benefits does your company provide?

	Yes	No	No Answer	Total
None	44	62	322	428
Health insurance	273	42	113	428
Life insurance	273	41	114	428
Other (please describe)				
_____	48	48	332	428

2.14 How do you account for the expense associated with these other post-retirement benefits?

	Health Insurance	Life Insurance	Other
(a) Pay as you go (*i.e.*, amount paid is expensed).	261	225	26
(b) Expense is accrued over employee's working lives.	3	27	15
(c) Terminal basis (*i.e.*, recording expense upon the retirement of the employee).	6	9	3
(d) Other method (please describe)			
_____	3	8	2
(e) DO NOT KNOW	1	2	0
No Answer	153	154	381
More than one answer	1	3	1
Total	428	428	428

2.15 How does your company fund these benefits?

	Health Insurance	Life Insurance	Other
(a) Pay as you go (*i.e.*, no advance funding).	264	218	36
(b) Advance funded (over the employee's career) through an insurance contract.	7	23	2

(c) Advance funded (over the employee's career) through
    another vehicle   4   16   6

(d) Terminal funding (*i.e.*, funding upon the retirement of
    the employee) through an insurance contract.   4   12   1

(e) Terminal funding (*i.e.*, funding upon the retirement of
    the employee) through another vehicle.   4   2   2

(f) Other method (please describe) _____   2   5   1

(g) DO NOT KNOW   0   0   0

No answer   143   147   378

More than one answer   0   5   2

Total   428   428   428

2.16 For 1979, did your company disclose the existence of other post-retirement benefits and related accounting policy in the notes to the financial statements?

21	312	95	428
Yes	No	No Answer	Total

2.17 Estimate the annual accounting expense and annual amount of benefit payments (expressed as a percent of the payroll for active employees covered by all pension plans) for providing post-retirement:

(a) Health insurance

Expense

106	21	11	4	286	428
1% Or Less	1% To 3%	3% To 6%	Over 6%	No Answer	Total

Payments

110	16	13	4	285	428
1% Or Less	1% To 3%	3% To 6%	Over 6%	No Answer	Total

(b) Life insurance

Expense

117	14	3	0	294	428
1% Or Less	1% To 3%	3% To 6%	Over 6%	No Answer	Total

Payments

112	15	5	0	296	428
1% Or Less	1% To 3%	3% To 6%	Over 6%	No Answer	Total

(c) Other post-retirement
    benefits (please describe)

Expense

15	4	1	1	407	428
1% Or Less	1% To 3%	3% To 6%	Over 6%	No Answer	Total

Payments

15	4	1	0	408	428
1% Or Less	1% To 3%	3% To 6%	Over 6%	No Answer	Total

2.18 Have you ever estimated the present value of the obligation for post-retirement benefits other than pensions?

69	244	15	99	1	428
Yes	No	DNK	No Answer	More Than One Answer	Total

SECTION III

User Data

This Section Should Only Be Answered By "Users" Of Financial Statements (Commercial Bankers, Financial Analysts, Investment Advisers, Insurance Carriers, Etc.)

Please indicate your response by checking the appropriate box.

3.01 Generally, how familiar are you with the accounting requirements under APB No. 8 for the cost of pension plans?

Very familiar	8
Somewhat familiar	12
Not very familiar	7
Not at all familiar	1
No answer	400
Total	428

3.02 For what major purpose are your analyses of pension accounting information used? (Please check only one box.)

Credit decisions	10
Investment decisions	14
Economic research	0
Investment banking	0
Other (please describe)	
	4
No answer	399
More than one answer	1
Total	428

3.03 When analyzing companies that sponsor pension plans, how useful to you is the pension accounting information that is presently made available pursuant to APB No. 8?

Very useful	1
Somewhat useful	15
Not very useful	11
Not useful at all	0
No answer	400
More than one answer	1
Total	428

3.04 Regardless of how useful presently available pension accounting information is in reaching your conclusion, how often do you incorporate this type of information in your analyses?

Incorporate into all analyses	5
Incorporate into most analyses	3
Incorporate into some analyses	14
Incorporate into very few or none	6
No answer	400
Total	428

3.05 To what extent has pension accounting data affected your analyses and decisions regarding specific companies? (Please rank in terms of frequency, with one being most frequent.)

No effect	7
Confirmed other data	10
Tempered conclusions which otherwise would have been reached	4
Substantially altered conclusions	1
Reversed conclusions	0
No answer	405
More than one answer	1
Total	428

SECTION IV

Perception of the Issues

In order to evaluate specific financial reporting issues relating to accounting for pension costs (including disclosure matters), a number of basic concepts are addressed here.

For each of the following statements please indicate whether you: Strongly Agree (SA), Agree (A), Feel Neutral (N), Disagree (D), Strongly Disagree (SD), or Do Not Know (DNK).

Methodology

4.01 The methods and techniques used in accounting for pension costs by the sponsoring employer should **generally** be:

(a) Consistent with those used in accounting by the plan, as required by SFAS No. 35.

60	215	33	55	30	19	16	428
SA	A	N	D	SD	DNK	No Answer	Total

(b) Consistent with those used for funding purposes.

67	209	35	69	26	6	16	428
SA	A	N	D	SD	DNK	No Answer	Total

(c) Consistently applied with respect to each of the company's defined benefit plans.

108	202	29	44	21	5	18	1	428
SA	A	N	D	SD	DNK	No Answer	More Than One Answer	Total

(d) Consistent with those used by other employers maintaining defined benefit plans.

37	119	83	101	66	4	18	428
SA	A	N	D	SD	DNK	No Answer	Total

Ongoing vs. Terminating Plan

4.02 In accounting for pension costs by the sponsoring employer, it should generally be assumed that the plan is:

(a) An ongoing entity.

253	154	1	6	0	0	14	428
SA	A	N	D	SD	DNK	No Answer	Total

(b) Going to terminate during or at the end of the current accounting period.

2	12	6	124	255	2	27	428
SA	A	N	D	SD	DNK	No Answer	Total

4.03 Please indicate the importance of each of the following items, for financial reporting purposes, in assessing a sponsoring employer's pension costs. **Under the column "Rank,"** please rank each item in order of importance, using "1" for the most important item. If two or more items are equally important, use the same number for those items. **Under the column "Weight,"** indicate the relative importance of each item, using a scale of "1" to "6," with "1" meaning very important, "2" important, "3" useful, "4" of passing interest, "5" almost useless, and "6" completely useless or misleading.

Item	RNK 1	2	3	4	5	6	7	8	9	10	11	12	13	14	15	16	NO RNK	WT 1	2	3	4	5	6	NO WT
(a) Some measure of an obligation* and the value of plan assets.	188	62	42	30	23	5	8	7	12	5	5	2	3	4	0	0	32	216	91	47	15	12	8	39
(b) Pension expense for the period.	235	77	27	14	12	10	6	8	4	2	2	1	1	0	0	0	29	246	80	48	11	1	2	40
(c) Amount actually funded for the period.	78	59	70	34	38	30	26	14	14	10	9	4	4	0	2	0	36	112	107	91	51	14	13	40
(d) The net "charges" in the ERISA Funding Standard Account for the most recent plan year.	11	4	7	13	10	19	12	44	34	31	41	32	27	36	43	3	61	13	27	58	87	89	97	57
(e) Actuarial cost method and assumptions used for expense purposes.	51	52	75	65	36	32	25	17	10	10	7	7	3	2	1	0	35	99	123	93	40	15	13	45
(f) Actuarial cost method and assumptions used for funding purposes.	33	22	44	50	58	48	45	24	20	12	15	7	3	2	3	0	42	63	109	101	65	21	20	49

*The term "obligation" as used in this questionnaire generally means the actuarial present value of pension benefits payable in the future related to service already performed by employees. It is particularly important that this term be understood. Please see the Glossary for further explanation.

Item	1	2	3	4	5	6	7	8	9	10	11	12	13	14	15	16	NO RNK	1	2	3	4	5	6	NO WT
(g) Pension expense for the period expressed as:																								
(i) a percentage of payroll.	17	10	17	30	20	24	34	44	36	31	42	33	33	7	3	0	47	27	44	101	100	53	53	50
(ii) a percentage of pre-tax profits.	7	0	5	11	14	10	15	32	46	32	44	53	44	39	10	2	64	6	19	54	102	79	107	61
(iii) a percentage of total revenues.	4	0	2	14	6	13	18	29	41	29	45	42	43	33	38	3	68	4	13	50	100	79	120	62
(h) The rate the unfunded obligation is being amortized for expense purposes.	24	17	59	72	49	59	41	16	19	9	9	6	4	4	0	0	40	63	117	123	48	22	9	46
(i) The rate the unfunded obligation is being amortized for funding purposes.	14	12	24	37	46	62	75	32	25	18	14	11	7	4	3	0	44	37	84	133	73	29	23	49
(j) A statement that the unfunded obligation is being amortized for expenses purposes, and that the rate (or amount) of amortization is not expected to increase in future years.	7	5	7	18	27	30	25	50	62	39	28	34	26	18	3	0	49	14	40	85	96	75	71	47
(k) A statement that the unfunded obligation is being amortized for funding purposes, and that the rate (or amount) of amortization is not expected to increase in future years.	6	3	7	12	25	18	29	47	54	46	26	29	36	29	7	0	54	13	31	82	88	82	84	48

Item	1	2	3	4	5	6	7	8	9	10	11	12	13	14	15	16	NO RNK	1	2	3	4	5	6	NO WT
(l) Funding ratio—the obligation divided by plan assets.	11	7	9	12	16	24	19	36	34	38	40	29	26	45	28	1	53	21	26	94	98	71	69	49
(m) An estimate of pension contributions and expense for the next few years, expressed as a percent of payroll.	5	3	5	10	13	21	17	25	33	28	34	44	33	26	82	1	48	9	18	69	90	72	124	46
(n) Other (please describe).	10	2	2	1	1	1	2	1	1	0	0	0	1	0	1	1	404	9	3	4	1	1	0	410

SECTION V

Pension Cost Recognition

APB Opinion No. 8 provides for a **minimum** annual expense provision for pension cost equal to the total of (1) normal cost, (2) an amount equivalent to interest on unfunded prior service cost, and in some circumstances, (3) a supplemental provision for vested benefits. The **maximum** annual provision is generally the normal cost and 10 percent of prior service costs. Opinion No. 8 specifies five acceptable actuarial cost methods, as well as variations of those methods (see Glossary for a description of those methods).

Except in unusual circumstances, actuarial gains and losses are to be spread or averaged rather than accorded immediate recognition. From 10 to 20 years is considered a reasonable period over which to spread actuarial gains and losses. Opinion No. 8 also requires recognition of unrealized appreciation or depreciation in the value of investments on a systematic basis that avoids giving undue weight to short-term market fluctuations.

The Opinion does not require the recording of an overall pension obligation as a liability on the sponsoring employer's balance sheet.

For each of the following statements please indicate whether you: Strongly Agree (SA), Agree (A), Feel Neutral (N), Disagree (D), Strongly Disagree (SD), or Do Not Know (DNK).

Expense Measurement

5.01 The current APB Opinion No. 8 requirements for measurement of pension expense are appropriate and should not be changed.

18	150	81	131	26	16	6	428
SA	A	N	D	SD	DNK	No Answer	Total

5.02 The minimum expense provision should be modified to require amortization of unfunded past or prior service cost over a specified period (*i.e.*, 30 or 40 years) to conform with ERISA's minimum funding requirements.

50	250	65	46	8	5	4	428
SA	A	N	D	SD	DNK	No Answer	Total

5.03 The maximum expense provision should be modified to conform to ERISA's changes in the tax deduction limitation (*e.g.*, allow prior service cost to be amortized over a 10-year period, rather than at a rate of 10 percent per year).

47	207	92	57	10	11	4	428
SA	A	N	D	SD	DNK	No Answer	Total

5.04 With respect to the actuarial cost method used to calculate expense:

(a) Current APB Opinion No. 8 requirements should be retained.

26	210	76	70	16	25	5	428
SA	A	N	D	SD	DNK	No Answer	Total

(b) One actuarial cost method should be prescribed.

15	49	38	151	161	9	5	428
SA	A	N	D	SD	DNK	No Answer	Total

(c) The same actuarial cost method used by the sponsoring employer in pension plan funding calculations should be required.

41	209	60	75	24	14	5	428
SA	A	N	D	SD	DNK	No Answer	Total

(d) Additional alternatives to those in Opinion No. 8 should be permitted.

10	70	136	127	43	37	5	428
SA	A	N	D	SD	DNK	No Answer	Total

(e) Fewer alternatives to those in Opinion No. 8 should be permitted.

18	77	106	160	38	19	10	428
SA	A	N	D	SD	DNK	No Answer	Total

5.05 With respect to actuarial assumptions:

(a) The current flexibility permitted in Opinion No. 8 should be retained.

68	240	29	59	10	15	7	428
SA	A	N	D	SD	DNK	No Answer	Total

(b) Specific **types** of actuarial assumptions should be prescribed (*e.g.*, interest, mortality, turnover, future salary increases, etc.)

14	119	45	127	107	10	6	428
SA	A	N	D	SD	DNK	No Answer	Total

(c) Specific **quantitative amounts** for actuarial assumptions should be prescribed (*e.g.*, an interest rate as prescribed by the Pension Benefit Guaranty Corporation).

4	45	34	143	185	11	6	428
SA	A	N	D	SD	DNK	No Answer	Total

(d) The same actuarial assumptions used by the sponsoring employer in pension plan funding calculations should be required.

33	212	51	83	25	16	7	1	428
SA	A	N	D	SD	DNK	No Answer	More Than One Answer	Total

(e) The following benefit level increases (*e.g.*, improvements in the plan's benefit formula), related to services already performed for non-pay related plans (plans with stated dollar benefit formulas), should be recognized in current expense calculations:

(1) Contractually committed increases.

53	251	25	37	12	41	9	428
SA	A	N	D	SD	DNK	No Answer	Total

(2) Anticipated increases following a pattern of increases in past years.

8	85	59	170	52	44	10	428
SA	A	N	D	SD	DNK	No Answer	Total

(3) Anticipated increases not related to any past pattern.

2	47	60	175	88	46	10	428
SA	A	N	D	SD	DNK	No Answer	Total

5.06 With respect to the treatment of actuarial gains and losses:

(a) Current Opinion No. 8 requirements should be retained.

18	243	73	60	5	23	6	428
SA	A	N	D	SD	DNK	No Answer	Total

(b) One time period and one method for amortizing or spreading or averaging should be required (*e.g.*, spreading over 15 years) where gains and losses are separately amortized rather than included in future normal costs.

4	97	69	183	48	19	8	428
SA	A	N	D	SD	DNK	No Answer	Total

(c) Greater leeway than now exists should be permitted.

6	43	144	176	26	25	8	428
SA	A	N	D	SD	DNK	No Answer	Total

(d) Gains and losses should be recognized immediately.

7	21	42	212	125	13	8	428
SA	A	N	D	SD	DNK	No Answer	Total

5.07 The expense provision should be equal to the amount funded.

15	139	55	137	66	10	6	428
SA	A	N	D	SD	DNK	No Answer	Total

5.08 The expense provision should be equal to the net charges in the funding standard account.

0	33	79	173	71	58	14	428
SA	A	N	D	SD	DNK	No Answer	Total

5.09 The expense provision should be equal to the change in the unfunded obligation for pension costs:

(a) Only if the obligation is recorded as a liability on the sponsor's balance sheet.

7	80	45	153	86	43	14	428
SA	A	N	D	SD	DNK	No Answer	Total

(b) In all circumstances.

4	22	38	184	130	36	14	428
SA	A	N	D	SD	DNK	No Answer	Total

(c) Never.

70	95	68	99	33	50	13	428
SA	A	N	D	SD	DNK	No Answer	Total

Recording an Obligation*

5.10 Some measure of the obligation should be recorded as a liability in the sponsoring employer's balance sheet.

22	101	36	147	112	5	5	428
SA	A	N	D	SD	DNK	No Answer	Total

5.11 Recording a pension obligation as a liability will generally have an effect on a company's credit rating, ability to raise capital, etc.:

49	239	43	59	8	25	5	428
SA	A	N	D	SD	DNK	No Answer	Total

The following questions should be answered **based on the premise** that some measure of the obligation is required to be recorded as a liability.

5.12 The obligation should be recorded:

(a) In total, with plan assets reflected as assets of the sponsor.

6	62	25	186	136	6	7	428
SA	A	N	D	SD	DNK	No Answer	Total

(b) Net of the fair market value of plan assets.

18	140	66	159	27	11	7	428
SA	A	N	D	SD	DNK	No Answer	Total

(c) Net of an actuarial value of plan assets.

16	148	78	138	18	19	11	428
SA	A	N	D	SD	DNK	No Answer	Total

5.13 The offsetting debit to the recorded liability should be reflected as a:

(a) Deferred charge with subsequent amortization.

27	237	40	69	25	18	11	1	428
SA	A	N	D	SD	DNK	No Answer	More Than One Answer	Total

(b) Charge to current income.

6	42	35	187	126	17	15	428
SA	A	N	D	SD	DNK	No Answer	Total

(c) Charge to retained earnings.

6	51	41	198	101	18	13	428
SA	A	N	D	SD	DNK	No Answer	Total

5.14 Any one of a number of methods to measure the obligation should be permitted so long as the method is disclosed.

18	199	46	110	41	4	9	1	428
SA	A	N	D	SD	DNK	No Answer	More Than One Answer	Total

5.15 If instead one specified measure of the obligation is required, it should be based on (check one):

PBGC guaranteed benefits.	36
Vested benefits.	197
Accumulated benefits (SFAS No. 35).	159
Other (please describe).	19
No answer	16
More than one answer	1
Total	428

5.16 The obligation should be measured by the same actuarial method the sponsor used to determine:

(a) The expense provision for the period.

40	270	28	55	17	8	10	428
SA	A	N	D	SD	DNK	No Answer	Total

*As indicated earlier, the term "obligation" as used in this questionnaire, generally means the actuarial present value of pension benefits payable in the future related to service already performed by employees. It is particularly important that this term be understood. Please see the Glossary for further explanation.

(b) Funding for the period.

19	204	47	103	40	7	8	428
SA	A	N	D	SD	DNK	No Answer	Total

* * *

Questions 6.03 to 6.10 deal further with the calculation of a pension obligation, but in the context of footnote disclosure. If you have indicated that you strongly agree (SA) or agree (A) with the statement in 5.09 that a liability should be recorded, your answers to Questions 6.03 to 6.10 will be treated as if you answered them in the context of calculation of an obligation to be recorded as a liability, unless you check the following box:

I believe the obligation should be recorded as a liability, but my answers to Questions 6.03 to 6.10 do not relate to calculation of that amount (they relate only to amounts to be disclosed).

57	371	428
Response	No Answer	Total

SECTION VI

Disclosures Regarding Pension Costs

APB Opinion No. 8

6.01 APB Opinion No. 8 requires that certain pension cost disclosures should be made in financial statements or their notes. For the following items currently required to be disclosed by Opinion No. 8, indicate your view, by checking the appropriate box, as to which items should or should not be required to be disclosed in the future.

	(1) Agree Strongly That Disclosure Should Be Required	(2) Agree That Disclosure Should Be Required	(3) Neutral	(4) Agree That Disclosure Should Not Be Required	(5) Agree Strongly That Disclosure Should Not Be Required	(6) Do Not Know	(7) No Answer	(8) More Than One Answer	(9) Total
(a) A statement that the pension plan exists, identifying or describing the employee groups covered.	215	192	8	5	0	0	7	1	428
(b) A statement of the company's pension accounting and funding policies.	170	221	22	7	1	0	7	0	428
(c) The expense provision for pension cost for the period.	169	227	14	10	1	0	7	0	428
(d) The actuarial present value of unfunded vested benefits.	117	207	51	34	10	1	8	0	428
(e) Significant matters affecting comparability for all periods presented, such as changes in accounting methods (e.g., actuarial cost methods), changes in circumstances (e.g., actuarial assumptions), or adoption or amendment of a plan.	140	224	38	17	2	0	7	0	428

FASB Exposure Draft and SFAS 36

6.02 As an interim measure pending completion of its comprehensive project on "Accounting by Employers for Pensions," the FASB issued an Exposure Draft, "Disclosure of Pension and Other Post-Retirement Benefit Information," which would require additional pension cost disclosures. In its final statement, SFAS 36, the FASB decided that—

(1) required disclosure of significant actuarial assumptions will be limited to the assumed interest rate,

(2) separate disclosure of information related to groupings of over- and under-funded plans will not be required, and

(3) annual benefit valuations for plans with more than 100 participants will not be required. Please indicate your view, by checking the appropriate box:

	(1) Agree Strongly That Disclosure Should Be Required	(2) Agree That Disclosure Should Be Required	(3) Neutral	(4) Agree That Disclosure Should Not Be Required	(5) Agree Strongly That Disclosure Should Not Be Required	(6) Do Not Know	(7) No Answer	(8) More Than One Answer	(9) Total
(a) The actuarial present value of accumulated benefits.	59	164	87	88	21	1	8	0	428
(b) The actuarial present value of vested benefits.	78	227	58	45	11	1	8	0	428
(c) The fair market value of the plan's net assets available for benefits.	75	220	58	55	11	2	7	0	428
(d) A description of significant actuarial assumptions and asset valuation methods used to determine (a), (b), and (c) above.	58	184	76	82	18	2	8	0	428
(e) The assumed rate of return used to determine (a) and (b).	52	184	87	75	17	1	11	1	428

(f) For employers with more than one ongoing plan, plans should be grouped as to those that have: (1) an actuarial present value of accumulated plan benefits in excess of net assets and (2) net assets available for benefits in excess of the actuarial present value of plan benefits.

20	114	116	108	41	18	11	0	428

Disclosure of Pension Obligation

Please indicate your view by checking whether you: Strongly Agree (SA), Agree (A), Feel Neutral (N), Disagree (D), Strongly Disagree (SD), or Do Not Know (DNK).

6.03 No disclosure of the obligation should be required.

12	40	32	218	117	1	8	428
SA	A	N	D	SD	DNK	No Answer	Total

6.04 A single measure of the obligation should be disclosed.

17	205	69	101	26	2	8	428
SA	A	N	D	SD	DNK	No Answer	Total

6.05 More than one measure of the obligation should be disclosed.

5	79	87	192	47	8	10	428
SA	A	N	D	SD	DNK	No Answer	Total

6.06 If a single measure of the obligation is required to be disclosed, it should be based on (check one):

(a) PBGC Guaranteed Benefits.

5	28	48	192	53	9	93	428
SA	A	N	D	SD	DNK	No Answer	Total

(b) Vested benefits.

21	190	43	96	8	6	63	1	428
SA	A	N	D	SD	DNK	No Answer	More Than One Answer	Total

(c) Unfunded past service costs, as historically required by the Securities and Exchange Commission.

4	42	60	167	52	8	95	428
SA	A	N	D	SD	DNK	No Answer	Total

(d) Accumulated benefits (SFAS No. 35).

17	135	59	112	21	10	73	1	428
SA	A	N	D	SD	DNK	No Answer	More Than One Answer	Total

(e) Other (please describe)

12	416	428
Response	No Answer	Total

6.07 If more than one measure of the obligation is required to be disclosed, disclosure of the actuarial present value of the following should be required:

(a) PBGC guaranteed benefits.

8	60	59	173	68	12	48	428
SA	A	N	D	SD	DNK	No Answer	Total

(b) Vested benefits.

30	290	39	24	4	5	36	428
SA	A	N	D	SD	DNK	No Answer	Total

(c) Unfunded past service costs, as historically required by the Securities and Exchange Commission.

6	123	75	122	53	9	40	428
SA	A	N	D	SD	DNK	No Answer	Total

(d) Accumulated benefits (SFAS No. 35)

22	193	64	76	25	13	35	428
SA	A	N	D	SD	DNK	No Answer	Total

(e) The obligation measured by the same actuarial method used by the company to determine the expense provision for the period.

13	210	61	69	20	19	36	428
SA	A	N	D	SD	DNK	No Answer	Total

(f) The obligation measured by the same actuarial method used by the company to determine funding for the period.

4	148	67	117	33	18	41	428
SA	A	N	D	SD	DNK	No Answer	Total

(g) Other (please specify).

10	418	428
Response	No Answer	Total

6.08 Actuarial assumptions used in calculating the obligation should be:

(a) Those used in calculating the expense provision.

SA	A	N	D	SD	DNK	No Answer	Total
31	276	38	50	12	6	15	428

(b) Those used in funding calculations.

SA	A	N	D	SD	DNK	No Answer	Total
18	194	48	117	28	3	20	428

(c) Those used in the calculation of accumulated benefits pursuant to SFAS No. 35.

SA	A	N	D	SD	DNK	No Answer	Total
23	148	80	98	19	35	25	428

(d) Left to the discretion of the company and its actuary.

SA	A	N	D	SD	DNK	No Answer	Total
40	146	55	122	39	3	23	428

(e) Specified by type (*e.g.*, interest rate).

SA	A	N	D	SD	DNK	No Answer	More Than One Answer	Total
7	118	76	155	38	9	24	1	428

(f) Specified in terms of quantitative amounts (*e.g.*, an interest rate prescribed by the PBGC).

SA	A	N	D	SD	DNK	No Answer	Total
2	45	68	183	93	12	25	428

6.09 Use of the following assumptions should be required:

(a) Interest.

SA	A	N	D	SD	DNK	No Answer	Total
81	274	23	24	9	5	12	428

(b) Turnover.

SA	A	N	D	SD	DNK	No Answer	Total
53	241	50	49	12	7	16	428

(c) Mortality.

SA	A	N	D	SD	DNK	No Answer	Total
63	268	34	35	7	5	16	428

(d) Retirement age.

SA	A	N	D	SD	DNK	No Answer	Total
60	273	34	35	8	5	12	428

(e) Salary increases related to services performed to date.

SA	A	N	D	SD	DNK	No Answer	Total
41	218	53	73	16	11	16	428

(f) Future benefit increases.

SA	A	N	D	SD	DNK	No Answer	Total
18	106	74	154	50	8	17	428

(g) Disability.

SA	A	N	D	SD	DNK	No Answer	Total
22	162	117	73	19	13	22	428

(h) Other (please describe).

Response	No Answer	Total
10	418	428

6.10 Plan assets to be disclosed, either separately or in determining an unfunded obligation, should be valued at:

(a) Cost.

SA	A	N	D	SD	DNK	No Answer	Total
1	14	51	232	92	3	35	428

(b) Fair market value.

SA	A	N	D	SD	DNK	No Answer	Total
59	204	49	77	16	3	20	428

(c) The value used by the actuary for the relevant pension valuation.

37	166	85	86	23	7	24	428
SA	A	N	D	SD	DNK	No Answer	Total

(d) Other (please describe)

6	422	428
Response	No Answer	Total

Other Disclosures

6.11 Each of the following items of disclosure reflect additional information about a company's pension plan. This information generally appears in Form 5500, the annual report/return that is filed with the Internal Revenue Service for each plan maintained by the sponsor. Note that this question relates to companies with many plans as well as to those with only one plan. Please respond by checking the appropriate box as to which items should or should not be disclosed in a company's financial statements or notes.

	(1) Agree Strongly That Disclosure Should Be Required	(2) Agree That Disclosure Should Be Required	(3) Neutral	(4) Agree That Disclosure Should Not Be Required	(5) Agree Strongly That Disclosure Should Not Be Required	(6) Do Not Know	(7) No Answer	(8) Total
Information About the Plan and Employees Covered:								
(a) A description of specific plan provisions, including benefits (retirement, death, and disability) provided, the nature of the benefit formula (career average, final pay, etc.), the eligibility, and vesting provisions.	16	81	40	196	90	6	5	428
(b) A description of the funding vehicle(s).	12	112	67	172	56	3	6	428
(c) Various categories of employees covered, such as number of active participants, retirees, terminated vested participants, and death beneficiaries.	7	63	67	211	74	0	6	428
(d) Federal income tax status of the plan — whether it is qualified with the IRS.	37	181	78	95	31	0	6	428
A Description of the Actuarial Method, Assumptions, and Asset Valuation Method:								
(e) Used to calculate pension expense.	34	183	59	122	22	1	7	428
(f) Used for actual funding.	19	127	89	147	33	1	12	428

	(1) Agree Strongly That Disclosure Should Be Required	(2) Agree That Disclosure Should Be Required	(3) Neutral	(4) Agree That Disclosure Should Not Be Required	(5) Agree Strongly That Disclosure Should Not Be Required	(6) Do Not Know	(7) No Answer	(8) Total
A Description of Methods of:								
(g) Amortizing unfunded obligations.	25	220	67	93	14	1	8	428
(h) Amortizing actuarial gains and losses.	19	162	91	127	16	3	10	428
Matters Relating to Contributions and Benefit Payments for the Periods Presented:								
(i) Employer contributions.	30	229	55	86	17	2	9	428
(j) Employee contributions, if any.	17	117	98	153	30	4	9	428
(k) Employer contributions expressed as a percent of payroll.	10	51	108	203	47	1	8	428
(l) Employee contributions, if any, expressed as a percent of payroll.	4	27	107	219	59	2	10	428
(m) Payments to retirees and beneficiaries.	2	57	102	210	43	1	8	428

	(1) Agree Strongly That Disclosure Should Be Required	(2) Agree That Disclosure Should Be Required	(3) Neutral	(4) Agree That Disclosure Should Not Be Required	(5) Agree Strongly That Disclosure Should Not Be Required	(6) Do Not Know	(7) No Answer	(8) Total
An Estimate of Future Contributions and Expense								
(n) An estimate of pension contributions and expense for the next few years, expressed as a percent of payroll.	5	30	62	186	136	1	8	428

SECTION VII

Special Issues

Plant Closings

APB Opinion No. 8 requires that actuarial gains or losses arising from a single occurrence not directly related to the operation of the pension plan be recognized immediately. An example of such an occurrence is a plant closing. In this connection, please indicate your view by checking whether you: Strongly Agree (SA), Agree (A), Feel Neutral (N), Disagree (D), Strongly Disagree (SD), or Do Not Know (DNK).

7.01 The APB Opinion No. 8 requirements should be unchanged.

21	168	78	92	16	47	6	428
SA	A	N	D	SD	DNK	No Answer	Total

7.02 More guidance is needed as to what constitutes such an occurrence, including guidance as to partial plant closings and substantial reductions of employees.

22	226	74	58	8	33	7	428
SA	A	N	D	SD	DNK	No Answer	Total

7.03 Rather than recognizing an actuarial gain or loss, any obligation for unfunded vested benefits related to participants in the plan should be charged to income.

6	99	73	151	41	46	12	428
SA	A	N	D	SD	DNK	No Answer	Total

7.04 With respect to retired participants:

(a) There should be no change in the accounting for participants from that plant who were already retired.

18	263	50	39	1	47	10	428
SA	A	N	D	SD	DNK	No Answer	Total

(b) Unfunded vested benefits should be charged to income upon the occurrence.

8	112	62	154	30	51	11	428
SA	A	N	D	SD	DNK	No Answer	Total

7.05 Specific methodology should be prescribed for valuing the plan assets related to a closed plant.

4	109	101	121	27	55	10	1	428
SA	A	N	D	SD	DNK	No Answer	More Than One Answer	Total

Business Combinations

APB Opinion No. 16 requires, in an acquisition accounted for under the purchase method, that a liability should be recorded in the amount of the greater of: (1) accrued pension cost computed in conformity with the accounting policies of the acquiring company or, (2) the unfunded vested benefits.

7.06 The accounting treatment required by Opinion No. 16 should be unchanged.

2	109	101	99	16	70	11	428
SA	A	N	D	SD	DNK	No Answer	Total

7.07 More guidance is needed as to what is meant by pension costs computed in conformity with the accounting policies of the acquiring company.

14	174	90	71	7	61	11	428
SA	A	N	D	SD	DNK	No Answer	Total

7.08 Opinion No. 16 should be changed to require recording the following as a liability (in lieu of the current principle of recording the greater of (1) or (2) above):

(a) Accrued pension costs computed in conformity with the accounting policies of the acquiring company.

1	85	88	135	23	67	29	428
SA	A	N	D	SD	DNK	No Answer	Total

(b) Obligation for unfunded vested benefits.

4	77	88	147	22	63	27	428
SA	A	N	D	SD	DNK	No Answer	Total

(c) Obligation for PBGC guaranteed benefits.

0	25	80	178	52	63	30	428
SA	A	N	D	SD	DNK	No Answer	Total

(d) Present value of accumulated benefits (SFAS No. 35).

8	62	87	141	35	66	29	428
SA	A	N	D	SD	DNK	No Answer	Total

(e) No liability.

12	39	68	157	57	65	30	428
SA	A	N	D	SD	DNK	No Answer	Total

(f) Other (please specify)

8	420	428
Response	No Answer	Total

7.09 If a liability is recorded, it should be reduced in subsequent periods by:

(a) Allocating it over a specified period.

5	121	74	138	16	43	31	428
SA	A	N	D	SD	DNK	No Answer	Total

(b) Reducing it as the obligation is funded.

21	239	57	51	5	37	18	428
SA	A	N	D	SD	DNK	No Answer	Total

Multiemployer Plans

7.10 Employer accounting for multiemployer defined benefit plans should be subject to the same accounting rules as single employer defined benefit plans.

20	164	58	52	38	81	15	428
SA	A	N	D	SD	DNK	No Answer	Total

Foreign Plans

7.11 Employer accounting for costs related to foreign defined benefit plans should be subject to the same accounting rules as domestic plans.

14	153	59	80	27	81	14	428
SA	A	N	D	SD	DNK	No Answer	Total

7.12 Does your company maintain any foreign plans?

179	198	26	25	428
Yes	No	DNK	No Answer	Total

SECTION VIII

Other Post-Retirement Benefits

The FASB Exposure Draft "Disclosure of Pension and Other Post-Retirement Benefit Information" would have required a plan sponsor to include a description of other post-retirement benefits provided to employees, a description of the accounting policies presently followed for these benefits and the cost of the benefits included in determining net income for the period. The Board decided not to include that requirement in the final statement—SFAS 36. The Board is, however, still planning to consider accounting and disclosure requirements for other post-retirement benefits in connection with its project on accounting by employers for pensions.

Disclosure

8.01 Indicate your view by checking the appropriate box.

Disclosure of the following should be required.

	(1) Agree Strongly That Disclosure Should Be Required	(2) Agree That Disclosure Should Be Required	(3) Neutral	(4) Agree That Disclosure Should Not Be Required	(5) Agree Strongly That Disclosure Should Not Be Required	(6) Do Not Know	(7) No Answer	(8) Total
(a) The existence of other post-retirement benefits.	22	178	74	111	31	5	7	428
(b) The accounting policy for those benefits.	15	142	93	134	32	5	7	428
(c) The cost of the benefits in determining net income for the period.	15	139	84	136	40	5	9	428
(d) Some measure on a present value basis of the obligation for these benefits, along with the actuarial methods and assumptions used.	11	95	83	163	64	5	7	428

Expense and the Obligation for Post-Retirement Benefits

For each of the following statements please indicate whether you: Strongly Agree (SA), Agree (A), Feel Neutral (N), Disagree (D), Strongly Disagree (SD), or Do Not Know (DNK).

8.02 The expense provision for these costs should be accounted for as follows:

(a) Pay as you go.

29	146	73	117	31	12	20	428
SA	A	N	D	SD	DNK	No Answer	Total

(b) Terminal funding basis.

1	12	84	228	59	17	27	428
SA	A	N	D	SD	DNK	No Answer	Total

(c) Accrued over the working lives of the participants.

18	101	89	146	36	12	26	428
SA	A	N	D	SD	DNK	No Answer	Total

(d) Treated in the same manner as pension costs.

9	117	80	146	35	16	25	428
SA	A	N	D	SD	DNK	No Answer	Total

(e) No one method should be required.

41	179	74	83	18	12	20	1	428
SA	A	N	D	SD	DNK	No Answer	More Than One Answer	Total

(f) Other (please specify)

6	422	428
Response	No Answer	Total

8.03 Some measure on a present value basis of the obligation for these benefits should be recorded as an accounting liability on the sponsor's balance sheet.

10	89	49	143	115	12	8	2	428
SA	A	N	D	SD	DNK	No Answer	More Than One Answer	Total

8.04 The actuarial assumptions used to calculate an obligation for post-retirement benefits should be:

(a) Left to the direction of the company and its actuary.

60	248	34	52	12	10	11	1	428
SA	A	N	D	SD	DNK	No Answer	More Than One Answer	Total

(b) Specified by type (*e.g.*, interest rate).

5	84	75	166	59	14	25	428
SA	A	N	D	SD	DNK	No Answer	Total

(c) Specified in terms of quantitative amounts (*e.g.*, a specific rate of interest).

1	37	66	196	89	16	23	428
SA	A	N	D	SD	DNK	No Answer	Total

(d) Other comments (please describe)

5	423	428
Response	No Answer	Total

Accumulated Plan Benefits

Benefits that are attributable under the provisions of a defined benefit plan to employees' service rendered to date. It includes benefits expected to be paid to (a) retired or terminated employees or their beneficiaries, (b) beneficiaries of deceased employees and (c) present employees or their beneficiaries. See also "Present Value of Accumulated Plan Benefits."

Actuarial Assumptions

Estimates of future events affecting pension cost; for example, mortality rate, employee turnover, compensation levels, investment earnings, retirement age, cost-of-living, etc.

Actuarial Cost Method (as described in APB Opinion No. 8)

A recognized actuarial technique used for establishing the amount and incidence of employer contributions and/or accounting charges for pension cost under a defined benefit pension plan.

1. **Accrued benefit cost method**—unit credit method

    Under the unit credit method, future service benefits (pension benefits based on service after the inception of a plan) are funded as they accrue—that is, as each employee works out the service period involved. Thus, the normal cost under this method for a particular year is the present value of the units of future benefit credited to employees for service in that year (hence unit credit). For example, if a plan provides benefits of $5 per month for each year of credited service, the normal cost for a particular employee for a particular year is the present value (adjusted for mortality and usually for turnover) of an annuity of $5 per month beginning at the employee's anticipated retirement date and continuing throughout his life.

    The past service cost under the unit credit method is the present value at the plan's inception date of the units of future benefit credited to employees for service prior to the inception date.

    The annual contribution under the unit credit method ordinarily comprises (1) the normal cost, and (2) an amount for past service cost. The latter may comprise only an amount equivalent to interest on the unfunded balance or may also include an amount intended to reduce the unfunded balance.

    As to an individual employee, the annual normal cost for an equal unit of benefit each year increases because the period to the employee's retirement continually shortens and the probability of reaching retirement increases; also, in some plans, the retirement benefits are related to salary levels, which usually increase during the years. As to the employees collectively, however, the step-up effect is masked, since older employees generating the highest annual cost are continually replaced by new employees generating the lowest. For a mature employee group, the normal cost would tend to be the same each year.

    The unit credit method is almost always used when the funding instrument is a group annuity contract and may also be used in trusteed plans and deposit administration contracts where the benefit is a stated amount per year of service. This method is not frequently used where the benefit is a fixed amount (for example, $100 per month) or where the current year's benefit is based on earnings of a future period.

2. **Projected benefit cost methods**

    As explained above, the accrued benefit cost method (unit credit method) recognizes the cost of benefits only when they have accrued (in the limited sense that the employee service on which benefits are based has been rendered). By contrast, the projected benefit cost methods look forward. That is, they assign the entire cost of an employee's projected benefits to past, present, and future periods. This is done in a manner not directly related to the periods during which the service on which the benefits are based has been or will be rendered. The principal projected benefit cost methods are discussed below.

    (a) Entry age normal method—under the age normal method, the normal costs are computed on the assumption (1) that every employee entered the plan (thus, entry age) at the time of employment or at the earliest time he would have been eligible if the plan had been in existence, and (2) that contributions have been made on this basis from the entry age to the date of the actuarial valuation. The contributions are the level annual amounts which, if accumulated at the rate of interest used in the actuarial valuation, would result in a fund equal to the present value of the pensions at retirement for the employees who survive to that time.

    Normal cost under this method is the level amount to be contributed for each year. When a plan is established after the company has been in existence for some time, past service cost under this method at the plan's inception date is theoretically the amount of the fund that would have been accumulated had annual contributions equal to the normal cost been made in prior years.

    In theory, the entry age normal method is applied on an individual basis. It may be applied, however, on an aggregate basis, in which case separate amounts are not determined for individual employees. Further variations in practice often encountered are (1) the use of an average entry age, (2) the use, particularly when benefits are based on employees' earnings, of a level percentage of payroll in determining annual payments and (3) the computation of past service cost as the difference between the present value of the employer's projected benefits and the present value of the employer's projected normal cost contributions. In some plans, the normal cost contribution rate may be based on a stated amount per employee. In other plans the normal cost contribution itself may be stated as a flat amount.

In valuations for years other than the initial year the past service cost may be frozen (that is, the unfunded amount of such cost is changed only to recognize payments and the effect of interest). Accordingly, actuarial gains and losses are spread into the future, entering into the normal cost for future years. If past service cost is not frozen, the unfunded amount includes the effects of actuarial gains and losses realized prior to the date of the valuation being made.

The annual contribution under the entry age normal method ordinarily comprises (1) the normal cost and (2) an amount for past service cost. The latter may comprise only an amount equivalent to interest on the unfunded balance or may also include an amount intended to reduce the unfunded balance.

The entry age normal method is often used with trusteed plans and deposit administration contracts.

(b) Individual level premium method—the individual level premium method assigns the cost of each employee's pension in level annual amounts, or as a level percentage of the employee's compensation, over the period from the inception date of a plan (or the date of his entry into the plan, if later) to his retirement date. Thus, past service cost is not determined separately but is included in normal cost.

The most common use of the individual level premium method is with funding by individual insurance or annuity policies. It may be used, however, with trusteed plans and deposit administration contracts.

In plans using individual annuity policies, the employer is protected against actuarial losses, since premiums paid are not ordinarily subject to retroactive increases. The insurance company may, however, pass part of any actuarial gains along to the employer by means of dividends. Employee turnover may be another source of actuarial gains under such insured plans, since all or part of the cash surrender values of policies previously purchased for employees leaving the employer for reasons other than retirement may revert to the company (or to the trust). Dividends and cash surrender values are ordinarily used to reduce the premiums payable for the next period.

The individual level premium method generates annual costs which are initially very high and which ultimately drop to the level of the normal cost determined under the entry age normal method. The high initial costs arise because the past service cost (although not separately identified) for employees near retirement when the plan is adopted is in effect amortized over a very short period.

(c) Aggregate method—the aggregate method applies on a collective basis the principle followed for individuals in the individual level premium method. That is, the entire unfunded cost of future pension benefits (including benefits to be paid to employees who have retired as of the date of the valuation) is spread over the average future service lives of employees who are active as of the date of the valuation. In most cases this is done by the use of a percentage of payroll.

The aggregate method does not deal separately with past service cost (but includes such cost in normal cost). Actuarial gains and losses enter into the determination of the contribution rate and, consequently, are spread over future periods.

Annual contributions under the aggregate method decrease, but the rate of decrease is less extreme than under the individual level premium method. The aggregate cost method amortizes past service cost (not separately identified) over the average future service lives of employees, thus avoiding the very short individual amortization periods of the individual level premium method.

The aggregate method may be modified by introducing past service cost. This technique results in the method often being referred to as the "frozen initial liability method." (Note also that any other method that involves the freezing of an actuarial liability may result in the method being referred to as the "frozen initial liability method.") If the past service cost is determined by the entry age normal method, the modified aggregate method is the same as the entry age normal method applied on the aggregate basis. If the past service cost is determined by the unit credit method, the modified aggregate method is called the attained age normal method (discussed below).

The aggregate method is used principally with trusteed plans and deposit administration contracts.

(d) Attained age normal method—the attained age normal method is a variant of the aggregate method or individual level premium method in which past service cost, determined under the unit credit method, is recognized separately. The cost of each employee's benefits assigned to years after the inception of the plan is spread over the employee's future service life. Normal cost contributions under the attained age normal method, usually determined as a percentage of payroll, tend to decline but less markedly than under the aggregate method or the individual level premium method.

As with the unit credit and entry age normal methods, the annual contribution for past service cost may comprise only an amount equivalent to interest on the unfunded balance or may also include an amount intended to reduce the unfunded balance.

The attained age normal method is used with trusteed plans and deposit administration contracts.

3. **Terminal funding**

Under terminal funding, funding for future benefit payments is made only at the end of an employee's period of active service. At that time the employer either purchases a single-premium annuity which will provide the retirement benefit or makes an actuarial equivalent contribution to a trust. (Note—This method is not acceptable for determining the provision for pension cost under APB No. 8.)

Actuarial Experience Gains (Losses)

The effects on actuarially calculated pension cost of deviations between actual prior experience and the actuarial assumptions used.

Actuarial Present Value

The value today of an amount or amounts to be paid or received in the future discounted at some interest rate and reflecting actuarial factors such as population decrements, salary scales, and retirement age.

Annual Cost

The total yearly cost assigned to a particular year by the actuarial cost method in use. **Annual cost** generally equals the normal cost plus an amortized portion of prior service costs. See also "Normal Cost," "Past Service Cost," and "Prior Service Cost."

Contributions

The actual amount of monies an employer (and sometimes employees) pays to a pension plan fund to provide promised benefits.

Defined Benefit Plan (Pension Plan)

A retirement plan that specifies a determinable pension benefit that is usually based on factors, such as age, years of service, and/or salary. Contributions are actuarially calculated. A Defined Benefit Plan is contrasted with a Defined Contribution Plan which specifies a determinable contribution and the ultimate benefit will vary according to the value of accumulated plan assets.

ERISA

The Employee Retirement Income Security Act of 1974. Also known as the 1974 Pension Reform Act.

Expense Provision

The amount of money charged against income in a period in the sponsoring employer company's income statement.

Fund

Used as a verb: to fund means to pay over contributions to a funding agency, such as a trust, insurance company, or both.

Used as a noun: a fund refers to assets accumulated in a funding agency to meet retirement obligations as they become due.

Multiemployer Plan

A pension plan which is generally maintained under a collective bargaining agreement to which more than one employer makes contributions.

Normal Cost

The yearly cost assigned to service related to a particular year. The yearly cost assignment is determined by the actuarial cost method in use. See also "Past Service Cost," "Prior Service Cost," and "Annual Cost."

Obligation

In general, it is the actuarial present value of pension benefits payable in the future related or allocated to service performed by employees to date. This term is purposefully broad and not precisely defined. More specific definitions of a pension obligation include the actuarial present value of: PBGC Guaranteed Benefits; Accrued Benefits, Vested Benefits, Accumulated Benefits (SFAS No. 35), and prior service cost (using a particular actuarial cost method).

Participant

This would include: individuals who are active and currently earning credited service under the pension plan, individuals who are retired or separated from employment and receiving benefits from the plan, and individuals who are retired or separated from employment and not presently receiving benefits but who are entitled to future benefits. For more information, see the instructions for Item 7 in the Annual Return/Report Form 5500.

PBGC

The Pension Benefit Guaranty Corporation.

PBGC Guaranteed Benefits

Those benefits guaranteed to plan participants by the PBGC in the event that a defined benefit pension plan terminates.

Past Service Cost

The pension cost assigned to service which was completed before the inception of a pension plan. The cost associated with service before plan inception is determined by the actuarial cost method in use. See also "Normal Cost," "Prior Service Cost," and "Annual Cost."

Pay As You Go

A method of recognizing cost when benefits are actually paid to plan participants.

Pension Plan

See "Defined Benefit Plan."

Plan Assets

See "Fund" (noun usage).

Plant Closing

The discontinued use of property, plant and/or equipment.

Present Value of Accumulated Benefits

This amount represents the actuarial present value of future benefits under a defined benefit plan's provisions based on employees' history of pay and service and other appropriate factors as of the date of computation. Actuarial assumptions are used to adjust the accumulated benefits to reflect the time value of money through discounts for interest and the probability of payment (by means of decrements such as for death, disability, withdrawal, or retirement) between the date of computation and the expected date of payment.

Prior Service Cost

The pension cost assigned to years prior to the date of a particular actuarial valuation, including any remaining past service cost and costs arising from pension benefit increases. The **Prior Service Cost** is determined by the actuarial cost method in use. See also "Normal Cost," "Past Service Cost," and "Annual Cost."

Unfunded Past Service Costs

Past service costs net of the value of the plan assets.

Unfunded Prior Service Costs

Prior service costs net of the value of the plan assets.

Unfunded Vested Benefits

The present value of vested benefits net of the value of the plan assets.

Vested Benefits

Benefits that are not contingent upon an employee's future service.

SEVEN

MODELING ANALYSES

INTRODUCTION

Chapter Five discussed major issues regarding accounting for pension costs. These issues are relevant to two basic questions:

- What obligation for pensions, if any, should be recognized as an accounting liability or disclosed on a plan sponsor's financial statements?
- How should the annual pension expense provision be determined?

This chapter presents a quantitative analysis of the alternative answers to these two questions.

PENSION OBLIGATION AND PENSION EXPENSE

Pension Obligation

This analysis considers eight alternative measures of pension obligation. The measures are organized into three categories, according to their underlying rationale, as follows:

- Category 1—Measures based on benefits accrued to date:
  - • PBGC guaranteed benefits.

- • Vested benefits.
- • Benefits at risk.
- • Accumulated benefits.

- Category 2—Measures based on allocation of projected benefit:
  - • Past service cost under the accrued benefit—salary prorate cost method (pro-rata allocation of projected benefit based on salary).
  - • Past service cost under the accrued benefit-service prorate cost method (pro-rata allocation of projected benefit based on service).

- Category 3—Measures based on allocation of *cost* of projected benefit:

  - • Past service cost under the entry age—constant percent of salary cost method.
  - • Past service cost under the entry age—constant amount cost method.

Omitted from Category 3 above are obligation measures based on some commonly used projected benefit cost methods—the aggregate method and the various frozen initial liability cost methods. These cost methods are not considered since they do not develop a past service cost which most actuaries would consider to be a valid measure of pension obligation.[1]

Pension Expense

Under the current accounting principles set forth in APB Opinion No. 8, pension expense is determined using an actuarial cost method. Total pension expense is comprised of:

- Normal cost;
- A provision for amortization of, or interest on, any unfunded past service cost; and
- A provision for actuarial gains or losses (not explicitly calculated under some cost methods).

For this analysis, pension expense is defined as normal cost plus 30-year amortization of any unfunded past service cost (unless noted otherwise). The effect of gains and losses on expense will be considered in the final section of the chapter.

The analysis of pension expense will consider the following actuarial cost methods:

- Accrued benefit cost method.

- Accrued benefit-salary prorate cost method.

- Accrued benefit-service prorate cost method.

- Entry age-constant percent of salary cost method.

- Entry age-constant amount cost method.

- Aggregate cost method.

Methodology

The analysis of the alternative methods of measuring pension obligation and expense has been made using a model consisting of these elements:

- Three model pension plans illustrating the three most common types of benefit formulas,
  - • A final pay plan providing 1% of final pay times years of service,
  - • A career average plan providing 1% of pay in each year of service,
  - • A unit benefit plan providing a fixed benefit amount for each year of service;

- Three model plan populations consisting of active members at a range of ages, years of service and salaries as well as retired and terminated vested members, which exhibit differing characteristics of growth, stability and decline over a 50-year period; and

- A set of actuarial assumptions used for valuing the model pension plan obligation and expense.

From these elements, the computer is used to project pension obligation and expense for each year of the 50-year period.

In order to study the impact of the various factors that determine obligation and expense, changes are made to the various elements of the model, and the 50-year projections are repeated.

This model, as do most models, contains certain simplifications. Much of the modeling analysis assumes that the actual experience of a plan is exactly as predicted by actuarial assumptions, so that no actuarial gains or losses occur.

Excluding gains and losses does not significantly affect the meaningfulness of the modeling results. The focus of the analysis is on the comparison of different obligation measures or cost methods. The relationships which exist between the obligations produced by alternative measures, or the pension expense produced by alternative cost methods, will tend to remain constant, regardless of whether gains or losses have occurred in the past.

In addition, much of the analysis considers patterns of obligation and expense over an extended period (50 years). Assuming that the actuarial assumptions are in fact the actuary's "best estimate," there is no reason to expect that either gains or losses will predominate. Considered over a long period then, using a model in which experience follows assumptions should give a reasonable approximation of the patterns of obligation and expense which might actually result.

Over the short term, actuarial gains or losses can significantly affect pension obligation and expense. The impact of gains and losses on obligation, expense and the sponsor's financial statements is considered in the final section of this chapter.

A detailed description of the model is given in Appendix A.

Organization Of The Analysis

The analysis is generally structured around the factors that impact plan cost identified in Chapter Three:

- Plan provisions,
- Nature and experience of the plan membership,
- Actuarial assumptions, and
- Actuarial methods.

The analysis will specifically focus on these questions:

- How do pension obligation and expense differ among the alternative methods of measuring obligation and expense?

- How is the pattern of pension obligation and expense influenced by the nature of the plan membership?

- How is the pattern of pension obligation and expense influenced by the plan's benefit formula?

- How are pension obligation and expense influenced by actuarial assumptions?

- How are company financial statements impacted by alternative accounting treatments described in Chapter Five (e.g., booking an unfunded obligation as a liability)?

Most of the analysis focuses on the model final pay plan. However, unless otherwise noted, the observations drawn from the analysis are also applicable to other types of plan benefit formulas.

A summary of significant findings and observations relating to each question is given, followed by supporting data. In addition, since the final pay plan is used for the majority of the analysis, Appendix B provides detailed results of the modeling projections for this plan.

This chapter uses the quantitative results of a specific model in order to observe more general relationships concerning pension obligation as measured by alternative obligation measures and pension expense as measured by alternative cost methods. Use of a different model would yield different quantitative results; however, the observations drawn from the modeling data are applicable to a broad range of defined benefit pension programs.

HOW DO PENSION OBLIGATION AND EXPENSE DIFFER AMONG THE ALTERNATIVE METHODS OF MEASURING OBLIGATION AND EXPENSE?

Impact of Measurement Method on Pension Obligation

The pension obligations produced by the alternative measures were analyzed using the model. Pension obligation was determined throughout the 50-year projection period for the model final pay pension plan and the stationary active population projection (Table 3 in Appendix A).

Observations

- Alternative obligation measures produce pension obligations that vary widely. The table below shows the obligation under each measure as a percentage of the accumulated benefits obligation and as a percentage of annual employee compensation for years 1 and 50 of the projection.

Obligation Measure	Percentage of Accumulated Benefits Obligation		Percentage of Employee Compensation	
	Year 1	Year 50	Year 1	Year 50
PBGC guaranteed benefits	—	86%	—	76%
Vested benefits	89%	96%	30%	86%
Accumulated benefits	100%	100%	34%	89%
Benefits at risk	102%	101%	34%	90%
Past service cost—				
• Accrued benefit—salary prorate cost method	118%	107%	40%	95%
• Accrued benefit—service prorate cost method	158%	122%	53%	108%
• Entry age—constant percent of salary cost method	202%	138%	68%	123%
• Entry age—constant amount cost method	230%	149%	77%	133%

Comparison of Final Pay Plan Obligation Under Alternative Measures for Years 1 and 50 of Stationary Plan Population Projection.

Supporting Data

Table 1 in Appendix B shows the final pay plan pension obligation under each measurement method at 10-year intervals throughout the projection period. Comparison of years 1 and 50 shows that differences are greatest for new plans with no retired or terminated vested members (year 1), since obligations for these members are the same under all measurement methods.

Note that the PBGC guaranteed benefits measure produces no obligation in the first year. This is a result of the PBGC phase-in rules, which state that benefits arising upon inception or amendment of a plan are initially not guaranteed, but come under PBGC coverage at the rate of 20% per year.

Note also that with the exception of PBGC guaranteed benefits, all of the alternative obligations are calculated using a 7% interest assumption. The PBGC guaranteed benefits obligation is based on a variable interest assumption which, in the aggregate, exceeds 7%. As a result, in this model the PBGC guaranteed benefits measure produces the lowest obligation. Comparison of the PBGC guaranteed benefits obligation with other obligation measures must take into account the interest assumptions used with each measure.

IMPACT OF MEASUREMENT METHOD ON NORMAL COST AND PENSION EXPENSE

Using the same model (final pay pension plan and the stationary active population projection), the normal cost and pension expense produced by the various actuarial cost methods are analyzed.

Observations

The table on page 154 shows the normal cost as a percentage of compensation developed by the various cost methods. Since the active population in this illustration is identical in makeup from year to year, these normal cost rates under all cost methods with the exception of the aggregate remain constant throughout the 50-year projection. The table also shows the initial past service cost in the first year and total pension expense at intervals throughout the projection period.

Supporting Data

Figure A shows total expense from the table above as a percent of employee compensation. Note that while the accrued benefit cost method has the highest normal cost rate (4.3% of compensation), it also produces the lowest past service cost. As a result, the total expense provision of normal cost plus amortization of the past service cost is lowest initially under the accrued benefit cost method.

COST METHODS
(Amounts in 000's)

	Accrued Benefit		Accrued Benefit – Salary Prorate		Accrued Benefit – Service Prorate		Entry Age – Constant Percent of Salary		Entry Age – Constant Amount		Aggregate	
Normal Cost Percentage	4.3%		4.2%		4.0%		3.7%		3.5%		10.9%-4.0%	
Past Service Cost	$9,140		$10,770		$14,400		$18,460		$21,050		—	
Pension Expense*/Percent of Annual Compensation												
Year 1	$1,870	6.9%	$1,970	7.2%	$2,170	8.0%	$2,390	8.8%	$2,540	9.5%	$2,970	10.9%
10	2,520	6.0	2,600	6.2	2,760	6.6	2,930	7.0	3,050	7.3	2,860	6.8
30	5,500	5.0	5,520	5.0	5,490	5.0	5,450	4.9	5,440	4.9	4,780	4.3
50	12,640	4.3	12,380	4.2	11,590	4.0	10,670	3.7	10,140	3.5	11,600	4.0

*Normal cost plus 30-year amortization of past service cost.

Comparison of Final Pay Plan Normal Cost, Past Service Cost and Expense Under Alternative Cost Methods and Stationary Plan Population Projection.

In later years, the amortization component represents a continuously declining proportion of total expense. After 30 years, the past service cost is fully amortized, and pension expense consists solely of normal cost.

The patterns of expense exhibited in Figure A are typical of a population that remains constant in character and experiences no actuarial gains or losses. A consistent pattern of actuarial losses would slow, or even reverse, the pattern of declining expense (as a percentage of compensation) shown in the first 30 years of Figure A, and would produce a rising, rather than level, pattern of expense after year 30. Repeated actuarial gains would have the opposite effect.

The effect which a changing plan population has on pension expense is explored in the next section.

HOW IS THE PATTERN OF PENSION OBLIGATION AND EXPENSE INFLUENCED BY THE NATURE OF THE PLAN MEMBERSHIP?

This section considers the effect of different plan populations on the relationships between pension obligation and expense measured by the alternative obligation measures and cost methods. The model for this analysis is the final pay pension plan and the plan populations described in Tables 3, 4 and 5 of Appendix A. As discussed in the Appendix, these populations represent plan memberships which are at various times immature (membership shifted toward young, low-service employees), mature (stable distribution of active, retired and terminated vested members) and overmature (membership shifted toward retired and terminated vested members and older, active members).

Impact of Plan Population on Pension Obligation

Observations
- Obligation measures based on allocation of the cost of projected plan benefits (e.g., past service cost under the entry age cost methods) produce

156

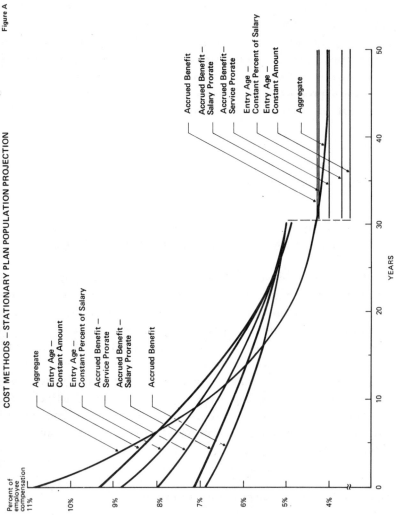

FINAL PAY PLAN PENSION EXPENSE AS PERCENTAGE OF COMPENSATION UNDER ALTERNATIVE
COST METHODS – STATIONARY PLAN POPULATION PROJECTION

Figure A

the largest pension obligation, and obligation measures based on benefits accrued to date produce the smallest obligation, regardless of the nature and experience of the population, provided there are active members in the population.

• As a population matures, the pension obligation as measured by a given method will increase as a percent of employee compensation. Using the accumulated benefits measure, pension obligation in the model ranges from 39% to 195% of annual compensation as the population varies from an immature to an overmature state. If the obligation is measured by the entry age-constant percent of salary past service cost, the obligation varies from 63% to 253% of annual compensation for populations which are immature and overmature, respectively.

• While pension obligation under any measure will increase as a percentage of active employee compensation as a plan population matures, some obligation measures are more sensitive than others to changes in the nature of the population. Measures based on benefits accrued to date show a proportionately greater increase in obligation as a population ages than do other obligation measures. For example, as the population in the model varies from an immature to an overmature state, the vested benefits obligation increases from 35% to 193% as a percentage of compensation, an increase by a factor of 5.5. The past service cost under the entry age-constant percent of salary cost method increases from 63% to 253% as a percentage of compensation, an increase by a factor of 4.0.

Supporting Data

The chart on page 158 shows the final pay plan pension obligation produced by the alternative measures as a percentage of the accumulated benefits obligation for immature, mature and overmature populations. The immature population is shown in year 10 of Table 4 of Appendix A. The mature and overmature populations are shown in year 50 of Tables 3 and 4 of Appendix A, respectively. Each obligation is also shown as a percentage of annual employee compensation. The proportionate increase in obligation as a percentage of compensation as the population progresses from an immature to an overmature state is included.

Obligation Measure	Percentage of Accumulated Benefits Obligation			Percentage of Employee Compensation			Ratio of Overmature Population Percentage to Immature Population Percentage
Population:	Immature	Mature	Overmature	Immature	Mature	Overmature	
PBGC guaranteed benefits	80%	86%	88%	31%	76%	172%	5.5:1
Vested benefits	90%	96%	99%	35%	86%	193%	5.5:1
Accumulated benefits	100%	100%	100%	39%	89%	195%	5.0:1
Benefits at risk	102%	101%	100%	40%	90%	196%	4.9:1
Past service cost—							
• Accrued benefit—salary prorate cost method	110%	107%	105%	43%	95%	206%	4.8:1
• Accrued benefit—service prorate cost method	133%	122%	118%	52%	108%	230%	4.4:1
• Entry age—constant percent of salary cost method	162%	138%	129%	63%	123%	253%	4.0:1
• Entry age—constant amount cost method	181%	149%	136%	71%	133%	266%	3.7:1

Comparison of Final Pay Plan Obligation Under Alternative Measures for Three Differing Plan Populations.

Impact of Plan Population on the Pattern of Normal Cost and Pension Expense

Observations

- If a plan population is sufficiently immature, the accrued benefit cost methods produce the lowest normal costs.

- As an active population progresses from an immature to a mature and then overmature state, the accrued benefit cost methods result in a rising pattern of normal cost. The rate of increase is particularly sharp for the accrued benefit and the accrued benefit-salary prorate cost methods. Total pension expense may decline at first as a percentage of compensation, but will ultimately show a rising pattern.

- Unlike the accrued benefit methods, the entry age cost methods produce a level pattern of normal cost and a level or declining pattern of expense as a percentage of compensation.

- If an active population reaches and maintains a mature state in which the distribution of members tends to remain constant from year to year, all of the cost methods ultimately produce normal costs which are level as a percentage of compensation. Total pension expense will also begin to level out as a percentage of compensation as a higher percentage of the past service cost is funded. Note, however, that in actual practice periodic plan amendments increasing past service cost will often occur so that past service cost is never totally funded. Consequently, a pattern of expense may never be attained which is completely level as a percent of compensation.

Supporting Data

Figure B shows normal cost as a percent of compensation for the final pay plan under three representative cost methods using the declining population projection from Table 4 of Appendix A. The illustration begins at year 10, the point where the population is at its most immature state because numerous new members entered during years 1–10.

As the population ages, the accrued benefit and accrued benefit-

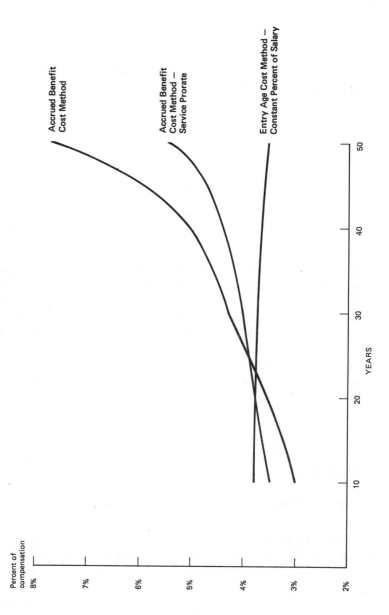

FINAL PAY PLAN NORMAL COST AS PERCENTAGE OF COMPENSATION
UNDER ALTERNATIVE COST METHODS —
DECLINING PLAN POPULATION PROJECTION

Figure B

Percent of
compensation

8%

7%

6%

5%

4%

3%

2%

10   20   30   40   50

YEARS

Accrued Benefit
Cost Method

Accrued Benefit
Cost Method —
Service Prorate

Entry Age Cost Method —
Constant Percent of Salary

service prorate cost methods produce a rising pattern of normal cost. The rate of the increase is especially rapid for the accrued benefit cost method. The entry age-constant percent of salary method, on the other hand, yields a normal cost pattern that is almost level.

Figure C shows the total pension expense (normal cost plus 30-year amortization of the past service liability) for the final pay plan under the three cost methods from Figure B. Pension expense under the entry age-constant percent of salary cost method declines up to year 30, and then remains almost level as a percent of compensation.[2] After year 30, the past service obligation is completely amortized, and pension expense consists solely of normal cost.

The accrued benefit-service prorate method shows a declining pattern of expense to year 30, although not as sharp as the entry age method. Expense then increases as a percentage of compensation. The accrued benefit cost method shows an increasing pattern of expense even before the past service cost is completely amortized.

Figures D and E show normal cost and expense for the three cost methods when the population projection is the growing active population (Table 5 of Appendix A). Now, as the active population approaches a mature state, normal cost and expense level out under all three methods. The rising patterns exhibited by the accrued benefit methods with an aging population are no longer present.

Most pension plans have active populations that are relatively mature or immature. Particularly in the case of a growing business, an immature population will often develop as new hires exceed the number of employees leaving each year, resulting in a large number of young, low-service plan members.

Overmature populations are most often found in declining industries where there is little hiring of new employees, and the work force gradually declines through attrition. For these populations, the accrued benefit cost methods produce a sharply rising pattern of expense, often at a time when the plan sponsor is least able to bear it.

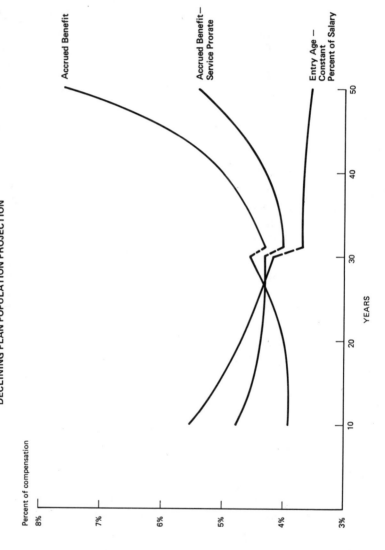

Figure C

FINAL PAY PLAN PENSION EXPENSE AS PERCENTAGE OF
COMPENSATION UNDER ALTERNATIVE
COST METHODS —
DECLINING PLAN POPULATION PROJECTION

Percent of compensation

8%

7%

6%

5%

4%

3%

10   20   YEARS   30   40   50

Accrued Benefit

Accrued Benefit—
Service Prorate

Entry Age —
Constant
Percent of Salary

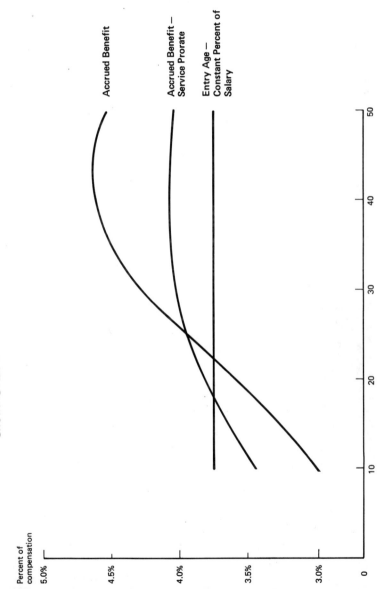

FINAL PAY PLAN NORMAL COST AS PERCENTAGE OF COMPENSATION
UNDER ALTERNATIVE COST METHODS —
GROWING PLAN POPULATION PROJECTION

Figure D

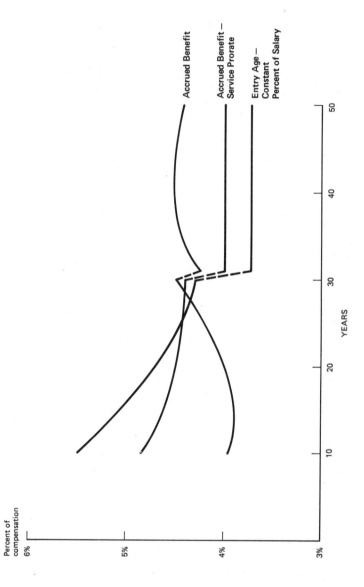

Figure E

FINAL PAY PLAN PENSION EXPENSE AS PERCENTAGE OF
COMPENSATION UNDER ALTERNATIVE
COST METHODS —
GROWING PLAN POPULATION PROJECTION

Accrued Benefit

Accrued Benefit —
Service Prorate

Entry Age —
Constant
Percent of Salary

Percent of
compensation

6%

5%

4%

3%

10   20   30   40   50

YEARS

HOW IS THE PATTERN OF PENSION OBLIGATION AND EXPENSE INFLUENCED BY THE PLAN'S BENEFIT FORMULA?

Defined benefit pension plans display a diverse array of formulas for determining plan benefits. Most plans, however, have a benefit formula that can be classified as one of three types:

- Final pay formula—benefit based on a percentage of the member's salary in the years just prior to retirement.

- Career average formula—benefit based on a percentage of each year's salary over the course of the member's active career.

- Unit benefit formula—benefit based on a fixed amount for each year of active employment, independent of salary.

This section will consider the impact of the plan benefit formula on pension obligation and pension expense. The analysis will compare the obligation and expense arising under each of the three model plans described in Table 1 of Appendix A. The model provides for annual amendments to the career average and unit benefit plans, so that the three plans pay out equivalent benefits to retired and vested employees. Accordingly, the next question for the analysis is: What differences in pension obligation and expense occur solely because of differences in the plan benefit formulas?

Impact of Plan Formula on Pension Obligation

The model population for the analysis will be the stationary active population (Table 3 of Appendix A). Rather than attempting to show obligation for each of the alternative measures, one measure from each category is illustrated. The three measures selected are the accumulated benefits measure and the past service cost under the accrued benefit-service prorate and entry age-constant percent of salary cost methods.

Observations

- Obligation measures based on benefits accrued to date (with the exception of PBGC guaranteed benefits) produce the same pension obligation regardless of plan type. The PBGC guaranteed benefits obligation for the career average and unit benefit plans will be slightly less than the final pay plan obligation due to the phase-in rules for plan amendments.

• Measuring the obligation as the past service cost under the accrued benefit-service prorate cost method, pension obligations for the career average and unit benefit plans are 14% and 18% less than the final pay plan obligation, respectively, when the population has reached a mature status.

• Measuring pension obligation as the past service cost under the entry age-constant percent of salary cost method, pension obligations for the career average and unit benefit plans are 19% and 24% less than the final pay plan obligation, respectively, when the population has reached a mature status.[3]

Supporting Data

Table 1 shows pension obligation for the final pay, career average and unit benefit plans as measured by the three representative obligation measurement methods. The table shows that each plan has the same obligation as measured by the accumulated benefits measure. This is true of any of the measures based on benefits accrued to date, with the exception of the PBGC guaranteed benefits. The annual amendments to the career average and unit benefit plans increase each plan member's accrued benefit so that the accrued benefits under the three plans are always equal. Since the accrued benefits are equal, these measures produce equal pension obligations.

The PBGC guaranteed benefits measure does not produce equal obligation amounts because of the PBGC phase-in rules on new plans and plan amendments. The career average and unit benefit plans are amended each year to increase accrued benefits, and these increases must be phased in over subsequent five-year periods. As a result, PBGC guaranteed benefits under the final pay plan slightly exceed those under the other two plans.

Table 1 also shows that when the pension obligation is based on allocation of projected plan benefits (past service cost under the accrued benefit-service prorate cost method) or allocation of the cost

TABLE 1

COMPARISON OF PENSION OBLIGATION UNDER
THREE DIFFERING PLAN FORMULAS AND THREE REPRESENTATIVE
OBLIGATION MEASURES
(Amounts in 000's)

Year	Accumulated Benefits All Plans	Past Service Cost Accrued Benefit – Service Prorate Cost Method					Past Service Cost Entry Age – Constant Percent of Salary Cost Method				
		Final Pay	Career Average	%*	Unit Benefit	%*	Final Pay	Career Average	%*	Unit Benefit	%*
1	$ 9,140	$ 14,400	$ 10,220	71%	$ 9,140	63%	$ 18,460	$ 12,200	66%	$ 10,540	57%
10	28,180	36,310	29,850	82%	28,180	78%	42,570	32,910	77%	30,340	71%
20	56,150	69,330	58,860	85%	56,150	81%	79,490	63,830	80%	59,660	75%
30	96,870	118,240	101,260	86%	96,870	82%	134,710	109,320	81%	102,550	76%
40	159,440	194,100	166,560	86%	159,440	82%	220,800	179,630	81%	168,660	76%
50	259,130	315,310	270,660	86%	259,130	82%	358,600	291,860	81%	274,070	76%

*Percent of corresponding final pay plan obligation. Data based on the stationary plan population projection, years 1–50.

of projected plan benefits (past service cost under the entry age-constant percent of salary cost method), the final pay plan obligation exceeds the career average and unit benefit plan obligations.

This disparity occurs because a member's projected final pay plan benefit will always exceed his projected benefit under the other two plans. Only if the effect of future plan amendments is included in the calculation of the career average and the unit benefit plan projected benefits will the projected benefits, and hence the pension obligations, for the three plans be equal.

Thus under some obligation measures, differences in pension obligation will arise among plans which provide equivalent benefits, simply because of differences in the benefit formulas through which these benefits are provided. Including an assumption of future plan amendments in the calculation of pension obligation could eliminate these differences; however, there are a number of arguments, both practical and philosophical, against including such an assumption in measuring pension obligations.[4]

The data shown in Table 1 is based on a model in which plan amendments occur annually so that accrued benefits under the career average and unit benefit plans always keep pace with the final pay plan. As a practical matter, plans are amended less frequently and on a less precise basis. The fact remains that in comparing pension obligations between final pay plans, which automatically relate benefits to compensation at retirement, and career average or unit benefit plans, which rely on periodic amendments to keep benefits in relation to pay at retirement, obligation measures based on accrued benefits will be much less sensitive to the benefit formula than will measures based on projected benefits.

Impact of Plan Benefit Formula on Pattern of Pension Expense

Alternative methods have been proposed for determining pension expense. Of particular interest is the treatment of past service cost arising upon plan inception and subsequent increases in past service cost arising upon plan amendment. Current accepted accounting practice calls for the amortization of the initial past service cost and subsequent increases at a rate not faster than 10% per year; in some cases the provision may consist of interest only on the unfunded past service cost. An alternative discussed in Chapter Five is to immediately expense the past service cost created when a plan is installed or amended. The analysis below considers the pattern of pension expense by plan type under three alternative methods of computing expense.

The model for the analysis consists of:

• The three model pension plans,

• The stationary plan population projection (Table 3 of Appendix A), and,

• Three representative cost methods:

   • • Accrued benefit,

   • • Accrued benefit-service prorate, and,

   • • Entry age-constant percent of salary.

Observations

• Under the accrued benefit cost method, there is little variation in pension expense by plan type when pension expense is defined as normal cost plus immediate expensing of the initial past service cost and any subsequent increases in past service cost arising out of plan amendments. When pension expense is defined as normal cost plus 10-year or 30-year amortization of the initial past service cost and subsequent increases, the career average and unit benefit plans show a pattern of pension expense that is lower than the final pay plan expense in the initial years and higher in the later years. The range of variation is shown below. Note that the amount of variation increases as the amortization period increases.

		Accrued Benefit Cost Method					
		Percentage of Final Pay Plan Expense					
		Career Average Plan			Unit Benefit Plan		
Pension Expense with:	Year:	1	30	31-50	1	30	31-50
Immediate expensing		95%	101%	101%	94%	101%	101%
10-year amortization		77%	105%	105%	76%	105%	105%
30-year amortization		71%	109%	111%	69%	110%	112%

Pension Expense for Career Average and Unit Benefit Plans as Percentage of Final Pay Plan Expense Under Accrued Benefit Cost Method and Alternative Methods of Expensing Past Service Cost.

• Under both the accrued benefit-service prorate and entry age-constant percent of salary cost methods, the career average and unit benefit plans show a pattern of pension expense that is lower than the final pay plan in the initial years and higher in later years, regardless of the method used to define expense. The amount of variation is least under the immediate expensing method and greatest under the 30-year amortization method. The range of variation under each cost method is shown below.

Pension Expense with:	Year:	Accrued Benefit – Service Prorate Cost Method					
		Percentage of Final Pay Plan Expense					
		Career Average Plan			Unit Benefit Plan		
		1	30	31-50	1	30	31-50
Immediate expensing		71%	107%	107%	63%	110%	110%
10-year amortization		70%	110%	110%	60%	115%	115%
30-year amortization		69%	106%	116%	59%	110%	122%

Pension Expense for Career Average and Unit Benefit Plans as Percentage of Final Pay Plan Expense Under Accrued Benefit-Service Prorate Cost Method and Alternative Methods of Expensing Past Service Cost.

Pension Expense with:	Year:	Entry Age – Constant Percent of Salary Cost Method					
		Percentage of Final Pay Plan Expense					
		Career Average Plan			Unit Benefit Plan		
		1	30	31-50	1	30	31-50
Immediate expensing		66%	113%	113%	57%	117%	117%
10-year amortization		66%	117%	117%	55%	122%	122%
30-year amortization		66%	108%	124%	54%	112%	132%

Pension Expense for Career Average and Unit Benefit Plans as Percentage of Final Pay Plan Expense Under Entry Age-Constant Percent of Salary Cost Method and Alternative Methods of Expensing Past Service Cost.

Supporting Data

Table 2 shows pension expense for the final pay, career average and unit benefit plans using the accrued benefit cost method. The analysis assumes immediate, 10- and 30-year expensing of the initial past service cost and increases in past service cost arising upon plan amendment. All three plans have an initial past service cost at plan inception. In addition, the career average and unit benefit plans have increases in past service cost each year due to annual amendments. Tables 3 and 4 show the same data using the accrued benefit-service prorate and entry age-constant percent of salary cost methods.

These tables show that, under some cost methods, very different patterns of expense can occur for plans that provide equivalent benefits. The accrued benefit cost method tends to produce equivalent patterns of pension expense when immediate expensing is used or when the amortization period for past service cost is not too long. The accrued benefit-service prorate and entry age-constant percent of salary cost methods produce significantly different patterns of expense, even under immediate expensing.

If the effect of future plan amendments is included in the determination of pension expense, expense for all three plans will be identical under the accrued benefit-service prorate and entry age-constant percent of salary cost methods. The previous section noted, however, the presence of strong arguments against an assumption of future amendments.

The patterns of expense shown in Tables 2–4 reflect a model in which annual amendments are made to the career average and unit benefit plans. If, as is typical, amendments occur less frequently, different patterns of expense would result. The significant observation remains that plans providing comparable benefits may display very different patterns of expense, particularly under certain cost methods and as the period for amortizing past service cost increases.

HOW ARE PENSION OBLIGATION AND EXPENSE INFLUENCED BY ACTUARIAL ASSUMPTIONS?

Chapter Three discussed the actuarial assumptions used in determining pension obligation and expense. While all of the assumptions play a role in these calculations, the salary increase and interest assumptions are particularly important. Changes in the mortality or turnover assumptions will generally have much less impact on pension obligation and expense than will changes in the salary

TABLE 2

PENSION EXPENSE UNDER ALTERNATIVE PLAN FORMULAS
ACCRUED BENEFIT COST METHOD
(Amounts in 000's)

Year	Immediate Expensing of Past Service Cost					Ten-Year Amortization of Past Service Cost					Thirty-Year Amortization of Past Service Cost				
	Final Pay	Career Average	%*	Unit Benefit	%*	Final Pay	Career Average	%*	Unit Benefit	%*	Final Pay	Career Average	%*	Unit Benefit	%*
1	$10,320	$ 9,770	95%	$ 9,740	94%	$ 2,400	$ 1,850	77%	$ 1,820	76%	$ 1,870	$ 1,320	71%	$ 1,290	69%
10	1,830	1,850	101%	1,850	101%	3,040	3,060	100%	3,060	100%	2,520	2,160	86%	2,130	85%
20	2,970	2,990	101%	3,000	101%	2,970	3,110	105%	3,120	105%	3,650	3,620	99%	3,620	99%
30	4,810	4,850	101%	4,860	101%	4,810	5,040	105%	5,050	105%	5,500	6,000	109%	6,040	110%
40	7,790	7,870	101%	7,870	101%	7,790	8,170	105%	8,190	105%	7,790	8,680	111%	8,740	112%
50	12,640	12,760	101%	12,770	101%	12,640	13,240	105%	13,280	105%	12,640	14,080	111%	14,180	112%

*Percent of corresponding final pay plan expense. Data based on stationary population projection, years 1-50.

TABLE 3

PENSION EXPENSE UNDER ALTERNATIVE PLAN FORMULAS
ACCRUED BENEFIT—SERVICE PRORATE COST METHOD

(Amounts in 000's)

Year	Immediate Expensing of Past Service Cost					Ten-Year Amortization of Past Service Cost					Thirty-Year Amortization of Past Service Cost				
	Final Pay	Career Average	%*	Unit Benefit	%*	Final Pay	Career Average	%*	Unit Benefit	%*	Final Pay	Career Average	%*	Unit Benefit	%*
1	$15,490	$10,950	71%	$ 9,740	63%	$ 3,000	$ 2,090	70%	$ 1,820	60%	$ 2,170	$ 1,500	69%	$ 1,290	59%
10	1,680	1,790	107%	1,850	110%	3,590	3,150	88%	3,060	85%	2,760	2,280	83%	2,130	77%
20	2,720	2,910	107%	3,000	110%	2,720	2,990	110%	3,120	115%	3,800	3,630	96%	3,620	95%
30	4,410	4,710	107%	4,860	110%	4,410	4,850	110%	5,050	115%	5,490	5,830	106%	6,040	110%
40	7,150	7,640	107%	7,870	110%	7,150	7,870	110%	8,190	115%	7,150	8,260	116%	8,740	122%
50	11,590	12,390	107%	12,770	110%	11,590	12,750	110%	13,280	115%	11,590	13,390	116%	14,180	122%

*Percent of corresponding final pay plan expense. Data based on stationary population projection, years 1–50.

TABLE 4

PENSION EXPENSE UNDER ALTERNATIVE PLAN FORMULAS
ENTRY AGE—CONSTANT PERCENT OF SALARY COST METHOD

(Amount in 000's)

Year	Immediate Expensing of Past Service Cost					Ten-Year Amortization of Past Service Cost					Thirty-Year Amortization of Past Service Cost				
	Final Pay	Career Average	%*	Unit Benefit	%*	Final Pay	Career Average	%*	Unit Benefit	%*	Final Pay	Career Average	%*	Unit Benefit	%*
1	$19,460	$12,870	66%	$11,030	57%	$ 3,460	$ 2,290	66%	$ 1,900	55%	$ 2,390	$ 1,590	66%	$ 1,290	54%
10	1,540	1,750	114%	1,810	118%	4,000	3,370	84%	3,200	80%	2,930	2,350	80%	2,140	73%
20	2,500	2,830	113%	2,930	117%	2,500	2,930	117%	3,060	122%	3,890	3,710	95%	3,650	94%
30	4,060	4,600	113%	4,750	117%	4,060	4,750	117%	4,970	122%	5,450	5,900	108%	6,100	112%
40	6,580	7,450	113%	7,700	117%	6,580	7,700	117%	8,050	122%	6,580	8,130	124%	8,680	132%
50	10,670	12,080	113%	12,480	117%	10,670	12,480	117%	13,060	122%	10,670	13,180	124%	14,080	132%

*Percent of corresponding final pay plan expense. Data based on stationary population projection, years 1-50.

increase or interest assumptions. Moreover, estimates on future mortality, turnover or age at retirement for an employee group can often be reasonably made based on past experience of the group or published data based on past experience of larger groups. Estimates on future salary increases and investment return are generally dependent on future economic events which are more difficult to predict. As a result, there has traditionally been much more variation in the salary increase and interest assumptions than in other, non-economic assumptions. It should be noted that of the alternative pension obligation measures, only the PBGC guaranteed benefits measure defines as part of the measurement method the actuarial assumptions to be used.[5]

The following analysis considers the impact of changes in the salary increase and interest assumptions on pension obligation and expense.

Impact of Salary Increase and Interest Assumptions on Pension Obligation

Up to this point, all actuarial computations have assumed 6% future salary increases and a 7% investment return. This section compares the effect of the following changes in assumptions on pension obligation:

- An increase in the salary assumption from 6% to 7%;

- An increase in the interest rate from 7% to 8%; and,

- A simultaneous 1% increase in both the salary and interest assumptions.

Observations

- A change in the salary assumption has no effect on pension obligation measures based on benefits accrued to date. Since accrued benefits depend only on past salaries, pension obligation under these measures is unaffected by any assumption as to future salaries.

- Increasing the salary assumption increases pension obligation under those measures which allocate the projected benefit or allocate the cost of the projected benefit. The degree of increase becomes less as the plan population matures.

- Both an increase in the interest assumption and a simultaneous increase in both the interest and salary assumptions produce a decrease in pension obligation when any of the three categories of obligation measures is used. As with the salary assumption, the effect of the change becomes less as the population matures.

- The table below summarizes the percentage increase (decrease) in pension obligation for the final pay plan under three representative obligation measures resulting from a 1% change in the salary and interest assumptions. The results are shown for years 1 and 50 from the stationary population projection (Table 3 of Appendix A).

	Accumulated Benefits		Past Service Cost Under Accrued Benefit-Service Prorate Cost Method		Past Service Cost Under Entry Age-Constant Percent of Salary Cost Method	
Population	*Immature*	*Mature*	*Immature*	*Mature*	*Immature*	*Mature*
Increase salary assumption from 6% to 7%	0%	0%	8%	4%	7%	4%
Increase interest rate from 7% to 8%	(13%)	(9%)	(14%)	(10%)	(13%)	(10%)
Increase salary and interest assumptions	(13%)	(9%)	(8%)	(7%)	(7%)	(7%)

Percentage Increase (Decrease) in Final Pay Plan Obligation Resulting from a Change in Salary and Interest Assumptions.

- An increase in the salary assumption has a much smaller impact on pension obligation under the career average plan than it does under the final pay plan. For the career average plan, an increase in the salary assumption from 6% to 7% produces a 1% to 2% increase in obligation measured as past service cost under the accrued benefit-service prorate cost method and results in virtually no change in the entry age-constant percent of salary past service cost obligation.

Supporting Data

Table 5 shows pension obligation for the final pay plan under the various salary and interest assumptions. The data is shown for the three representative obligation measures and the stationary plan populations in years 1 and 50 (Table 3 of Appendix A). The year 1 population has no retired or vested terminated members and shows a greater sensitivity to changes in the assumptions. The year 50 population is a very mature population with a large and stable distribution of retirees and vested terminations relative to active members. Most plan populations will have a distribution of active and inactive members somewhere between these two model populations. The effect of an increase in the salary assumption on the career average plan obligation is also shown for the same two populations.

Impact of Salary and Interest Assumptions on Pension Expense

The previous section analyzed the effect of the salary increase and interest assumption on pension obligation. This section will study the impact of these assumptions on normal cost and pension expense as measured by three representative cost methods. The model for the analysis is the final pay plan and the population in year 50 of the stationary population projection (Table 3 in Appendix A).

Observations

- The table below summarizes the percentage increase (decrease) in the final pay plan normal cost resulting from a 1% increase in the salary and interest assumptions.

COST METHODS

	Accrued Benefit	Accrued Benefit-Service Prorate	Entry Age-Constant Percent of Salary
Increase salary assumption from 6% to 7%	0%	11%	16%
Increase interest rate from 7% to 8%	(14%)	(17%)	(21%)
Increase salary and interest assumptions	(14%)	(8%)	(8%)

Percentage Increase (Decrease) in Final Pay Plan Normal Cost Resulting from a Change in Salary and Interest Assumptions.

TABLE 5

IMPACT OF SALARY AND INTEREST ASSUMPTIONS ON PENSION OBLIGATION
(Amounts in 000's)

Assumptions	Accumulated Benefits				Past Service Cost Accrued Benefit— Service Prorate Cost Method				Past Service Cost Entry Age—Constant Percent of Salary Cost Method			
Year	1	%*	50	%*	1	%*	50	%*	1	%*	50	%*
I. Final Pay Plan												
1. Model: 6%-salary; 7%-interest	$9,140	—	$259,130	—	$14,400	—	$315,310	—	$18,460	—	$358,600	—
2. 7%-salary; 7%-interest	9,140	0%	259,130	0%	15,600	8%	327,660	4%	19,720	7%	372,140	4%
3. 6%-salary; 8%-interest	7,980	(13%)	235,740	(9%)	12,340	(14%)	282,250	(10%)	15,980	(13%)	321,170	(10%)
4. 7%-salary; 8%-interest	7,980	(13%)	235,740	(9%)	13,270	(8%)	292,270	(7%)	17,080	(7%)	332,860	(7%)
II. Career Average Plan Assumptions												
1. Model: 6%-salary; 7%-interest	$9,140	—	$259,130	—	$10,220	—	$270,660	—	$12,200	—	$291,860	—
2. 7%-salary; 7%-interest	9,140	0%	259,130	0%	10,370	1%	272,260	1%	12,100	(1%)	290,810	0%

*Percentage increase (decrease) in corresponding obligation under model assumptions. Data based on immature and mature plan populations in years 1 and 50, respectively, of the stationary population projection.

• The impact of changes in the salary and interest assumptions on total
pension expense will vary according to the magnitude of any unexpensed
past service cost. In general, as the size of the unexpensed past service cost
becomes less, the impact of a change in assumptions increases. The table
below summarizes the percentage increase (decrease) in the final pay plan
expense resulting from a 1% increase in the salary and interest assumptions.

COST METHODS

	Accrued Benefit		Accrued Benefit- Service Prorate		Entry Age- Constant Percent of Salary	
% Past service cost funded	50%	75%	50%	75%	50%	75%
Increase salary assumption from 6% to 7%	0%	0%	9%	13%	11%	16%
Increase interest rate from 7% to 8%	(13%)	(19%)	(15%)	(24%)	(17%)	(27%)
Increase salary and interest assumptions	(13%)	(19%)	(8%)	(12%)	(8%)	(14%)

Percentage Increase (Decrease) in Final Pay Plan Expense (Normal Cost Plus 30-Year Amortization
of Unfunded Past Service Cost) Resulting from a Change in Salary and Interest Assumptions.

Supporting Data

Table 6 compares normal cost for the final pay plan under the
various salary and interest assumptions and the stationary plan
population in year 50.

Table 7 compares total pension expense under the different
assumptions. The data is based on the final pay plan with the year 50
stationary plan population and pension expense defined as normal
cost plus 30-year amortization of the unfunded past service cost.

An old rule of thumb states that: "Every 1% increase in the
interest assumption results in a 20% decrease in plan costs." Table 7
shows that the accuracy of this guideline is dependent upon such
factors as the cost method and the degree to which the past service
cost has been funded.

TABLE 6

IMPACT OF SALARY AND INTEREST ASSUMPTIONS
ON FINAL PAY PLAN NORMAL COST
(Amounts in 000's)

Assumptions	Accrued Benefit Cost Method	%*	Accrued Benefit— Service Prorate Cost Method	%*	Entry Age— Constant Percent of Salary Cost Method	%*
1. Model: 6%-salary; 7%-interest	$12,640	—	$11,590	—	$10,670	—
2. 7%-salary; 7%-interest	12,640	0%	12,880	11%	12,350	16%
3. 6%-salary; 8%-interest	10,910	(14%)	9,610	(17%)	8,440	(21%)
4. 7%-salary; 8%-interest	10,910	(14%)	10,620	(8%)	9,780	(8%)

*Percentage increase (decrease) in corresponding normal cost under model assumptions. Data based on final pay plan and mature population in year 50 of stationary population projection.

TABLE 7

IMPACT OF SALARY AND INTEREST ASSUMPTIONS
ON FINAL PAY PLAN PENSION EXPENSE

(Amounts in 000's)

Final Pay Plan Cost Methods	Assumptions						
	Model: 6%-salary; 7%-interest	7%-salary; 7%-interest	%*	6%-salary; 8%-interest	%*	7%-salary; 8%-interest	%*
Accrued Benefit							
— 50% funded	$22,390	$22,390	0%	$19,640	(13%)	$19,640	(13%)
— 75% funded	17,520	17,520	0%	14,320	(19%)	14,320	(19%)
Accrued Benefit—Service Prorate							
— 50% funded	$23,460	$25,690	9%	$19,860	(15%)	$21,980	(8%)
— 75% funded	17,530	19,750	13%	13,380	(24%)	15,210	(12%)
Entry Age—Constant Percent of Salary							
— 50% funded	$24,170	$26,880	11%	$20,110	(17%)	$22,410	(8%)
— 75% funded	17,420	20,130	16%	12,740	(27%)	15,040	(14%)

*Percentage increase (decrease) in corresponding expense under model assumptions. Data based on the final pay plan and mature population in year 50 of the stationary population projection.

HOW ARE COMPANY FINANCIAL STATEMENTS IMPACTED BY ALTERNATIVE ACCOUNTING TREATMENTS?

Pension obligation and expense have been shown to be dependent on the obligation measure or cost method, nature and experience of the plan membership, plan provisions, and actuarial assumptions. The effect of a pension plan on the sponsoring company's financial statements is determined not only by these factors but also by the accounting treatment given obligation and expense in recording or disclosing them on the balance sheet and income statement. (Alternative ways of accounting for pension obligation and expense were discussed in Chapter Five.) The purpose of this section is to illustrate the effect of various accounting alternatives on company financial statements for:

- A company with an existing plan;

- A company establishing a new plan; and

- A company that is amending its plan, changing the plan's actuarial assumptions or experiencing actuarial gains or losses.

The analysis considers the following alternative accounting treatments for pension obligation and expense:

- Method 1—Continue current accounting treatment under APB Opinion No. 8.

- Method 2—Institute a new accounting standard. Under this standard, the unfunded obligation is booked with an immediate charge to income, and pension expense in subsequent years is defined as the change for the year in the pension obligation, less the change in plan assets (excluding amounts actually funded). Changes in obligation due to plan amendments, actuarial gains or losses or changes in actuarial assumptions are treated as any other change in obligation and immediately charged to income.

- Method 3—Institute a new accounting standard. Under this standard, the unfunded obligation is booked with an offsetting deferred charge which is amortized over 30 years. Pension expense in subsequent years is defined as the change in pension obligation (excluding changes in obligation arising out of certain events as noted below), plus a provision for amortization of the initial deferred charge and any subsequent deferred charges, less the change in plan assets (excluding amounts funded). Changes in pension obligation due to plan amendments, actuarial gains or losses or changes in assumptions are not immediately reflected in expense but are offset by additional deferred charges or credits, which are also amortized.[6]

The analysis which follows compares the impact of these three alternative accounting treatments on the financial statements of a plan sponsor. For this comparison, financial statements were developed for a hypothetical manufacturing company with a workforce of 1,500 employees and an annual payroll of approximately $30 million. Recent financial statements of several large manufacturing companies were used as a guide in determining the relationships between the various entries on these illustrative financials. Appendix A describes in detail the assumptions underlying the sample statements.

Obviously, it is difficult to illustrate the expected effect of alternative accounting standards on the financial statements of sponsoring employers. In addition to factors already mentioned which directly affect the determination of pension obligation and expense, the financial position of the employer, the financial position of the plan and the nature of the employer's business can have a major impact on this analysis.

Impact of Accounting Methods on Company with an Existing Plan

In this analysis, the model final pay pension plan is considered over a three-year period. Data is drawn from the last three years of the stationary active population projection (Table 3 of Appendix A). It is assumed the plan is funded using the entry age-constant percent of salary cost method and that at the beginning of year 1 plan assets equal 60% of the entry age past service cost. The annual company contribution to the plan consists of normal cost plus a payment to amortize the unfunded past service cost over 30 years. The amount funded satisfies the requirements of APB Opinion No. 8 as an acceptable pension expense, and the company's practice is to expense this amount each year.

The chart on page 184 shows relevant data for the plan at the beginning of year 1 and at the end of each year over the three-year period.

184

	Company Contribution for Year	Plan Assets	Entry Age Past Service Cost	Unfunded Past Service Cost	Accumulated Benefits Obligation	Unfunded Accumulated Benefits Obligation
Beginning Fiscal Year 1	—	$18,610	$31,010	$12,400	$22,410	$3,800
End Fiscal Year:						
1	$1,850	$20,280	$32,550	$12,270	$23,520	$3,240
2	1,900	22,040	34,170	12,130	24,690	2,650
3	1,950	23,880	35,860	11,980	25,910	2,030

Final Pay Plan Pension Data for Sample Financial Statements. (Amounts in 000's.)

Tables 8 and 9 show comparative financial statements for the sponsoring company under the three accounting treatments described above. In Table 8, the pension obligation measure for those methods which record the unfunded obligation is the accumulated benefits obligation. In Table 9, the pension obligation measure is the past service cost under the plan's funding method, in this case the entry age-constant percent of salary cost method.

Observations

- If accounting standards are changed to require booking the unfunded obligation by an immediate charge to income, a company with an unfunded obligation could experience a large reduction in net income in the year in which the new standard is instituted. This is particularly true for plans funded under a projected benefit cost method if the obligation measure is defined as the past service cost under the funding method. In the model used for this analysis, net income was reduced by 12% and equity by 2% in year 1 when the obligation was measured by the accumulated benefits (Table 8). When the obligation measure was the past service cost under the plan's funding method (the entry age cost method), net income was reduced by 44% and equity was reduced by 7% (Table 9).

- The impact on the sponsor's financial statements in the year an unfunded obligation is recorded by an immediate charge to income will vary widely according to a number of factors. Two important factors are the funding status of the plan and the profitability of the plan sponsor. The illustrative statements shown in Tables 8 and 9 are based on a model in which plan assets are initially 60% of the entry age past service cost and net income under current accounting treatment is approximately 17% of stockholders' equity. The table below compares the reduction in net income and equity which occurs in the year an unfunded obligation is charged to income assuming different levels of plan funding and net income as a percentage of equity.

- Following implementation of the new accounting standard which immediately charges the unfunded obligation to income, pension expense in years 2 and 3 is lower (net income higher), relative to expense under current accounting standards.

- In the model used for this analysis, recording the unfunded obligation by an offsetting deferred charge produced pension expense equivalent to that produced under current accounting principles when the obligation

TABLE 8

COMPARATIVE FINANCIAL STATEMENTS FOR COMPANY WITH AN EXISTING PLAN— PENSION OBLIGATION MEASURED BY ACCUMULATED BENEFITS

(Amounts in 000's)

	Year 1			Year 2			Year 3		
	Current Treatment	Record Unfunded Obligation by Immediate Charge Against Income	Record Unfunded Obligation by Deferred Charge	Current Treatment	Record Unfunded Obligation by Immediate Charge Against Income	Record Unfunded Obligation by Deferred Charge	Current Treatment	Record Unfunded Obligation by Immediate Charge Against Income	Record Unfunded Obligation by Deferred Charge
Assets									
Current Assets	$181,300	$181,300	$181,300	$214,000	$214,000	$214,000	$256,700	$256,700	$256,700
Long-Term Assets	97,700	97,700	97,700	115,200	115,200	115,200	138,300	138,300	138,300
Deferred Charges	0	0	3,760	0	0	3,710	0	0	3,660
Total Assets	$279,000	$279,000	$282,760	$329,200	$329,200	$332,910	$395,000	$395,000	$398,660
Liabilities and Stockholders' Equity									
Current Liabilities	$ 61,400	$ 61,400	$ 61,400	$ 72,400	$ 72,400	$ 72,400	$ 86,900	$ 86,900	$ 86,900
Long-Term Liabilities	50,200	50,200	50,200	57,400	57,400	57,400	70,900	70,900	70,900
Unfunded Pension Obligation	0	3,240	3,240	0	2,650	2,650	0	2,030	2,030
Stockholders' Equity	167,400	164,160	167,920	199,400	196,750	200,460	237,200	235,170	238,830
Total Liabilities and Stockholders' Equity	$279,000	$279,000	$282,760	$329,200	$329,200	$332,910	$395,000	$395,000	$398,660
Income									
Revenue	$397,900	$397,900	$397,900	$457,600	$457,600	$457,600	$540,000	$540,000	$540,000
Pension Expense	1,850	5,090	1,330	1,900	1,310	1,360	1,950	1,330	1,380
Other Expense	368,200	368,200	368,200	423,700	423,700	423,700	500,250	500,250	500,250
Net Income	$ 27,850	$ 24,610	$ 28,370	$ 32,000	$ 32,590	$ 32,540	$ 37,800	$ 38,420	$ 38,370
Ratios									
Debt*/Equity	30%	33%	32%	29%	31%	30%	30%	31%	31%
Income/Equity	17%	15%	17%	16%	17%	16%	16%	16%	16%
Income/Revenue	7%	6%	7%	7%	7%	7%	7%	7%	7%

*Long-term liabilities and unfunded pension obligation.

TABLE 9

COMPARATIVE FINANCIAL STATEMENTS FOR COMPANY WITH AN EXISTING PLAN—
PENSION OBLIGATION MEASURED BY ENTRY AGE PAST SERVICE COST
(Amounts in 000's)

	Year 1			Year 2			Year 3		
	Current Treatment	Record Unfunded Obligation by Immediate Charge Against Income	Record Unfunded Obligation by Deferred Charge	Current Treatment	Record Unfunded Obligation by Immediate Charge Against Income	Record Unfunded Obligation by Deferred Charge	Current Treatment	Record Unfunded Obligation by Immediate Charge Against Income	Record Unfunded Obligation by Deferred Charge
Assets									
Current Assets	$181,300	$181,300	$181,300	$214,000	$214,000	$214,000	$256,700	$256,700	$256,700
Long-Term Assets	97,700	97,700	97,700	115,200	115,200	115,200	138,300	138,300	138,300
Deferred Charges	0	0	12,270	0	0	12,130	0	0	11,980
Total Assets	$279,000	$279,000	$291,270	$329,200	$329,200	$341,330	$395,000	$395,000	$406,980
Liabilities and Stockholders' Equity									
Current Liabilities	$ 61,400	$ 61,400	$ 61,400	$ 72,400	$ 72,400	$ 72,400	$ 86,900	$ 86,900	$ 86,900
Long-Term Liabilities	50,200	50,200	50,200	57,400	57,400	57,400	70,900	70,900	70,900
Unfunded Pension Obligation	0	12,270	12,270	0	12,130	12,130	0	11,980	11,980
Stockholders' Equity	167,400	155,130	167,400	199,400	187,270	199,400	237,200	225,220	237,200
Total Liabilities and Stockholders' Equity	$279,000	$279,000	$291,270	$329,200	$329,200	$341,330	$395,000	$395,000	$406,980
Income									
Revenue	$397,900	$397,900	$397,900	$457,600	$457,600	$457,600	$540,000	$540,000	$540,000
Pension Expense	1,850	14,120	1,850	1,900	1,760	1,900	1,950	1,800	1,950
Other Expense	368,200	368,200	368,200	423,700	423,700	423,700	500,250	500,250	500,250
Net Income	$ 27,850	$ 15,580	$ 27,850	$ 32,000	$ 32,140	$ 32,000	$ 37,800	$ 37,950	$ 37,800
Ratios									
Debt*/Equity	30%	40%	37%	29%	37%	35%	30%	37%	35%
Income/Equity	17%	10%	17%	16%	17%	16%	16%	17%	16%
Income/Revenue	7%	4%	7%	7%	7%	7%	7%	7%	7%

*Long-term liabilities and unfunded pension obligation.

		Obligation Measure			
		Accumulated Benefits		Past Service Cost Under Entry Age Cost Method	
Percent of Entry Age Past Service Cost Funded	Net Income (Current Accounting Treatment) as Percent of Equity	Percent Decrease in:		Percent Decrease in:	
		Net Income	Stock-holders' Equity	Net Income	Stock-holders' Equity
60%	17%	12%	2%	44%	7%
60%	10%	19%	2%	73%	7%
30%	17%	45%	7%	77%	13%
30%	10%	74%	7%	*	13%

*Net loss results for year.

Percent Decrease in Income and Stockholders' Equity in Year Unfunded Pension Obligation Charged Immediately to Income Relative to Income and Equity Under Current Accounting Treatment.

measure was the past service cost under the entry age cost method (the plan's funding method—see Table 9). When the obligation measure was accumulated benefits, this alternative treatment produced pension expense almost 30% lower than expense under current treatment (Table 8).

Supporting Data

Tables 8 and 9 compare company financial statements under current and alternative accounting treatments of pension obligation and expense. Under current treatment, the company expenses the amount funded each year (normal cost plus a provision for amortization of the unfunded entry age past service cost). Under the alternative treatment which charges the unfunded obligation immediately to income, pension expense in year 1 is equal to the unfunded obligation at the beginning of the year, plus the change in obligation during the year, less the change in plan assets for the year, excluding amounts contributed for the year.[7] After the initial year, pension expense is the change in obligation for the year, less the change in plan assets for the year, excluding amounts contributed for the year. The table below shows the calculation of pension expense under this alternative.

	Obligation Measure					
	Accumulated Benefits			**Past Service Cost Under Entry Age Cost Method**		
Year:	**1**	**2**	**3**	**1**	**2**	**3**
Change in Obligation						
(1) Obligation end of year	$23,520	$24,690	$25,910	$32,550	$34,170	$35,860
(2) Obligation end of prior year	—	23,520	24,690	—	32,550	34,170
(3) Net change = (1)–(2)	$23,520	$ 1,170	$ 1,220	$32,550	$ 1,620	$ 1,690
Change in Plan Assets (Excluding Amounts Funded)						
(4) Assets end of year	$20,280	$22,040	$23,880	$20,280	$22,040	$23,880
(5) Assets end of prior year	—	20,280	22,040	—	20,280	22,040
(6) Company contribution for year	1,850	1,900	1,950	1,850	1,900	1,950
(7) Net change = (4)–(5)–(6)	$18,430	($ 140)	($ 110)	$18,430	($ 140)	($ 110)
(8) Pension Expense = (3)–(7)	$ 5,090	$ 1,310	$ 1,330	$14,120	$ 1,760	$ 1,800

Calculation of Final Pay Plan Expense Under Accounting Alternative Which Records Unfunded Obligation by Immediate Charge to Income. Expense Determined as Net Change in Obligation. (Amounts in 000's.)

When the unfunded obligation is offset by a deferred charge, annual pension expense each year is the change in the obligation for the year (excluding changes in obligation due to plan amendments, a change in assumptions or gains or losses), plus a provision for amortization of any deferred charges or credits, less the change in plan assets for the year, excluding amounts contributed for the year. In addition to the initial deferred charge which offsets the unfunded obligation in year 1, subsequent increases in obligation due to actuarial losses, a change to more conservative assumptions, or plan amendments are also offset by deferred charges and amortized. Actuarial gains or a change to more liberal assumptions produce a deferred credit which is amortized to reduce pension expense. The table below shows the calculation of pension expense when the unfunded obligation is offset by a deferred charge.

	Obligation Measure					
	Accumulated Benefits			**Past Service Cost Under Entry Age Cost Method**		
Year:	1	2	3	1	2	3
Change in Obligation						
(1) Obligation end of year	$23,520	$24,690	$25,910	$32,550	$34,170	$35,860
(2) Obligation end of prior year	—	23,520	24,690	—	32,550	34,170
(3) Deferred charge (credit) established to offset obligation*	3,800	0	0	12,400	0	0
(4) Net change = (1)-(2)-(3)	$19,720	$ 1,170	$ 1,220	$20,150	$ 1,620	$ 1,690
Change in Plan Assets (Excluding Amounts Funded)						
(5) Assets end of year	$20,280	$22,040	$23,880	$20,280	$22,040	$23,880
(6) Assets end of prior year	—	20,280	22,040	—	20,280	22,040
(7) Company contribution for year	1,850	1,900	1,950	1,850	1,900	1,950
(8) Net change = (5)-(6)-(7)	$18,430	($ 140)	($ 110)	$18,430	($ 140)	($ 110)
(9) *Provision for Amortization of Deferred Charges (Credits)***	$ 40	$ 50	$ 50	$ 130	$ 140	$ 150
(10) *Pension Expense* = (4)-(8)+(9)	$ 1,330	$ 1,360	$ 1,380	$ 1,850	$ 1,900	$ 1,950

*Deferred charge established in year 1 equal to unfunded obligation (measured at beginning of year). In subsequent years, changes in obligation due to gains or losses, plan amendments or a change in actuarial assumptions would generate additional deferred charges or credits.

**Provision determined as level payment to amortize deferred charge (credit), reduced (increased) by interest on deferred charge (credit).

Calculation of Final Pay Plan Pension Expense Under Accounting Alternative Which Records Unfunded Obligation by Offsetting Deferred Charge. Expense Determined as Net Change in Obligation (Excluding Certain Changes in Obligation Offset by Deferred Items), Plus a Provision for Amortization of Deferred Charges (Credits). (Amounts in 000's.)

When the obligation measure is the past service cost under the funding method (Table 9), current treatment and offsetting the unfunded obligation by a deferred charge both produce the same pension expense each year. This occurs because the deferred charge under the latter method is equivalent to the unfunded past service cost, and the period for amortizing each is the same (30 years in both cases).

Booking Net Unfunded Obligation Versus Alternative of Booking Both Pension Obligation and Plan Assets

Tables 8 and 9 assume that the net unfunded pension obligation (if any) is recorded on the balance sheet. An alternative method books both the total pension obligation and plan assets. As before, any net unfunded obligation is expensed immediately or offset by a deferred charge and amortized.

Table 10 compares the effect on financial statements of recording only the net unfunded obligation *versus* recording total obligation and plan assets. The comparison is made using the alternative accounting standard which records the unfunded obligation by an immediate charge to income.

In this illustration, booking both pension obligation and plan assets has no effect on net income and net worth as compared to booking only the unfunded obligation. Recording both the total obligation and plan assets does alter the debt/equity ratio, and could alter other ratios relating income to assets or assets to liabilities. The degree to which various ratios might be affected may depend on how the assets and obligation are recorded on the balance sheet (e.g., as current or long-term items).

Note that whether the plan assets and the total obligation are booked separately or on a net basis, a plan with assets exceeding the pension obligation will result in negative pension expense and increased income in the year the items are booked under immediate expensing or, alternatively, will generate a deferred credit to offset the excess assets, with amortization of this credit reducing pension expense in subsequent years.

TABLE 10

IMPACT ON FINANCIAL STATEMENTS OF RECORDING NET UNFUNDED OBLIGATION (WITH IMMEDIATE CHARGE AGAINST INCOME) VERSUS RECORDING TOTAL OBLIGATION AND PLAN ASSETS— PENSION OBLIGATION MEASURED BY ENTRY AGE PAST SERVICE COST

(Amounts in 000's)

	Year 1			Year 2			Year 3		
	Current Treatment	Book Net Unfunded Obligation	Book Obligation and Plan Assets	Current Treatment	Book Net Unfunded Obligation	Book Obligation and Plan Assets	Current Treatment	Book Net Unfunded Obligation	Book Obligation and Plan Assets
Assets									
Current Assets	$181,300	$181,300	$181,300	$214,000	$214,000	$214,000	$256,700	$256,700	$256,700
Long-Term Assets	97,700	97,700	97,700	115,200	115,200	115,200	138,300	138,300	138,300
Plan Assets	0	0	20,280	0	0	22,040	0	0	23,880
Total Assets	$279,000	$279,000	$299,280	$329,200	$329,200	$351,240	$395,000	$395,000	$418,880
Liabilities and Stockholders' Equity									
Current Liabilities	$ 61,400	$ 61,400	$ 61,400	$ 72,400	$ 72,400	$ 72,400	$ 86,900	$ 86,900	$ 86,900
Long-Term Liabilities	50,200	50,200	50,200	57,400	57,400	57,400	70,900	70,900	70,900
Unfunded/Total Pension Obligation	0	12,270	32,550	0	12,130	34,170	0	11,980	35,860
Stockholders' Equity	167,400	155,130	155,130	199,400	187,270	187,270	237,200	225,220	225,220
Total Liabilities and Stockholders' Equity	$279,000	$279,000	$299,280	$329,200	$329,200	$351,240	$395,000	$395,000	$418,880
Income									
Revenue	$397,900	$397,900	$397,900	$457,600	$457,600	$457,600	$540,000	$540,000	$540,000
Pension Expense	1,850	14,120	14,120	1,900	1,760	1,760	1,950	1,800	1,800
Other Expense	368,200	368,200	368,200	423,700	423,700	423,700	500,250	500,250	500,250
Net Income	$ 27,850	$ 15,580	$ 15,580	$ 32,000	$ 32,140	$ 32,140	$ 37,800	$ 37,950	$ 37,950
Ratios									
Debt*/Equity	30%	40%	53%	29%	37%	49%	30%	37%	47%
Income/Equity	17%	10%	10%	16%	17%	17%	16%	17%	17%
Income/Revenue	7%	4%	4%	7%	7%	7%	7%	7%	7%

*Long-term liabilities and (unfunded) pension obligation.

Impact on Company Establishing a New Plan

Significant pension obligation may occur when a new plan is installed if benefit credit is given for employee service prior to the date the plan is established. This section will consider the effect of alternative accounting methods on a company establishing a new plan.

Observations

- The initial obligation arising upon implementing the model final pay, career average and unit benefit plans ranged from approximately 30% to 70% of annual employee salaries, depending on the plan type and obligation measure.

- Requiring immediate expensing of the initial pension obligation at inception of the final pay plan results in a first year pension expense which is over four times the pension expense under current accounting rules.

Supporting Data

The chart below shows the initial pension obligation created upon inception of the three model plans, as measured by three different obligation measures. (Relevant data from Table 1 is repeated.)

	Accumulated Benefits	Past Service Cost Accrued Benefit – Service Prorate Cost Method	Past Service Cost Entry Age – Constant Percent of Salary Cost Method
Final pay plan	$9,100,000	$14,400,000	$18,500,000
Career average plan	9,100,000	10,200,000	12,200,000
Unit benefit plan	9,100,000	9,100,000	10,500,000

Initial Pension Obligation at Plan Inception by Plan Type.

The above data is based on the initial membership of 1,500 active employees in year 1 of the 50-year population projection shown in

Table 3 of Appendix A. Total salaries for this group are $27,200,000. Depending on the plan type and obligation measure, the initial obligation at plan inception represents $6,100 to $12,300 per employee or 33% to 68% of total annual salaries.

The chart below compares pension expense in the first three years of the final pay plan under the three accounting methods described earlier. The plan is funded using the entry age-constant percent of salary cost method. The annual contribution is normal cost plus 30-year amortization of the past service cost. Under current practice, the amount funded is the expense for the year, satisfactory under APB Opinion No. 8. The obligation measure is the accumulated benefits for the two accounting alternatives which record the initial obligation.

	Pension Expense (in 000's)		
Year:	1	2	3
Method 1—Expense amount funded—current practice.	$2,390	$2,440	$2,490
Method 2—Record initial obligation with immediate charge to income.	$10,870	$1,750	$1,760
Method 3—Record initial obligation with offsetting deferred charge.	$1,830	$1,850	$1,870

Pension Expense in Three Years Following Inception of Final Pay Plan Under Alternative Accounting Treatments.

The large, first-year expense under Method 2 represents the initial accumulated benefits obligation at inception of the plan ($9,100,000), plus the net increase in the obligation during year 1. By spreading out the expensing of the initial entry age past service cost of $18,500,000 through amortization, current accounting practice avoids a large initial expense in year 1. Offsetting the accumulated benefits obligation by a deferred charge accomplishes the same goal, as the deferred charge is amortized over 30 years. (In this illustration, Methods 1 and 3 do not produce equal expense since expense under current accounting practice is the annual contribution calculated under the entry age cost method, while expense under Method 3 is based on the accumulated benefits obligation and changes in this obligation.)

Impact of Actuarial Gains or Losses, Plan Amendments or Changes in Actuarial Assumptions

Actuarial gains and losses, plan amendments and changes in actuarial assumptions are all events that result in unanticipated changes in pension obligation and expense. This final section of the analysis quantifies the change in obligation resulting from a typical occurrence of such events and illustrates the resulting impact on pension expense under alternative accounting methods.

Observations

- Changes in pension obligation due to gains or losses, plan amendments or a change in actuarial assumptions can be significant items when measured against annual pension expense. Current accounting treatment spreads these increases or decreases in obligation to avoid wide fluctuations in annual expense.

- Requiring immediate expensing of changes in pension obligation can result in a very uneven pattern of expense. Actuarial losses, a change to more conservative assumptions and plan amendments increasing benefits may result in large increases in pension expense in a single year. Actuarial gains or a change to more liberal assumptions may result in a greatly reduced, or even negative, pension expense.

- An alternative to immediately charging all changes in pension obligation to income is to establish a deferred charge or deferred credit to offset the change in obligation arising out of gains or losses, a change in assumptions or plan amendments. Amortization of this charge or credit would then spread the change in obligation just as under current accounting treatment.

Supporting Data

Table 8 showed the impact of three accounting methods on the financial statements of a company with an ongoing plan. In Table 8, pension expense under current practice was the amount funded for the year, calculated using the entry age cost method. Pension expense under the two alternatives which record the unfunded obligation is based on the change in the accumulated benefits obligation. The chart below summarizes relevant data relating to year 1 of this illustration.

	Pension Expense				
Current Practice	Record Unfunded Obligation by Immediate Charge Against Income	Record Unfunded Obligation by Offsetting Deferred Charge	Accumulated Benefits Obligation	Plan Assets	Unfunded Obligation
$1,850	$5,090	$1,330	$23,520	$20,280	$3,240

Final Pay Plan Pension Expense and Accumulated Benefits Obligation in Year 1 From Table 8. (Amounts in 000's.)

Assume that at the end of year 1 plan assets have lost 5% of their value (i.e., assets are $19,266,000 instead of $20,280,000). This represents an actuarial loss for the year of $1,014,000. Table 11 shows financial statements for years 1 to 3, using the three alternative accounting methods.

Under current accounting practice the actuarial loss is amortized over 15 years beginning in year 2. (The 15-year amortization period, chosen arbitrarily, is the required period for amortizing gains and losses under ERISA's minimum funding standards.) Similarly, under the accounting alternative which offsets the unfunded obligation by a deferred charge, the actuarial loss is also offset by a deferred charge which is amortized over 15 years beginning in year 2. (See Note 7.)

Under the accounting treatment which immediately expenses the change in obligation, the full loss of $1,014,000 is expensed in year 2. As a result, the pension expense of $2,400,000 is 83% larger than the pension expense of $1,310,000 which would occur had there been no loss.[8]

Had plan assets gained 5% of their value at the end of year 1, an actuarial gain of $1,014,000 would have occurred. Under current practice, or under the alternative which offsets gains by a deferred credit, pension expense would include a negative provision representing amortization of this gain or credit each year for 15 years. Under the immediate expensing alternative, pension expense in year 2 would reflect the full amount of the gain.

A change in actuarial assumptions or a plan amendment can result in a change in pension obligation of even larger magnitude than the actuarial loss illustrated in Table 11.

TABLE 11

COMPARATIVE FINANCIAL STATEMENTS FOR COMPANY WITH AN EXISTING PLAN EXPERIENCING AN ACTUARIAL LOSS— PENSION OBLIGATION MEASURED BY ACCUMULATED BENEFITS

(Amounts in 000's)

	Year 1			Year 2			Year 3		
	Current Treatment	Record Unfunded Obligation by Immediate Charge Against Income	Record Unfunded Obligation by Deferred Income	Current Treatment	Record Unfunded Obligation by Immediate Charge Against Income	Record Unfunded Obligation by Deferred Charge	Current Treatment	Record Unfunded Obligation by Immediate Charge Against Income	Record Unfunded Obligation by Deferred Charge
Assets									
Current Assets	$181,300	$181,300	$181,300	$213,900	$213,900	$213,900	$256,500	$256,500	$256,500
Long-Term Assets	97,700	97,700	97,700	115,200	115,200	115,200	138,300	138,300	138,300
Deferred Charges	0	0	3,760	0	0	4,680	0	0	4,590
Total Assets	$279,000	$279,000	$282,760	$329,100	$329,100	$333,780	$394,800	$394,800	$399,390
Liabilities and Stockholders' Equity									
Current Liabilities	$ 61,400	$ 61,400	$ 61,400	$ 72,400	$ 72,400	$ 72,400	$ 86,900	$ 86,900	$ 86,900
Long-Term Liabilities	50,200	50,200	50,200	57,400	57,400	57,400	70,900	70,900	70,900
Unfunded Pension Obligation	0	3,240	3,240	0	3,640	3,640	0	2,990	2,990
Stockholders' Equity	167,400	164,160	167,920	199,300	195,660	200,340	237,000	234,010	238,600
Total Liabilities, and Stockholders' Equity	$279,000	$279,000	$282,760	$329,100	$329,100	$333,780	$394,800	$394,800	$399,390
Income									
Revenue	$397,900	$397,900	$397,900	$457,600	$457,600	$457,600	$540,000	$540,000	$540,000
Pension Expense	1,850	5,000	1,330	2,000	2,400	1,480	2,050	1,400	1,490
Other Expense	368,200	368,200	368,200	423,700	423,700	423,700	500,250	500,250	500,250
Net Income	$ 27,850	$ 24,610	$ 28,370	$ 31,900	$ 31,500	$ 32,420	$ 37,700	$ 38,350	$ 38,260
Ratios									
Debt*/Equity	30%	33%	32%	29%	31%	30%	30%	32%	31%
Income/Equity	17%	15%	17%	16%	16%	16%	16%	16%	16%
Income/Revenue	7%	6%	7%	7%	7%	7%	7%	7%	7%

*Long-term liabilities and unfunded pension obligation.

The chart below summarizes the change in the entry age past service cost and the accumulated benefits obligation which would accompany:

- An increase at the beginning of year 2 in the interest assumption from 7% to 8%, and,

- A plan amendment at the beginning of year 2 increasing the final pay formula from 1% of final pay for each year of service to 1.1% of final pay.

	Change in Entry Age Past Service Cost	Change in Accumulated Benefits Obligation
Increase interest as- sumption	($3,400,000)	($2,120,000)
Increase plan formula by amendment	$1,790,000	$ 890,000

Change in Final Pay Plan Entry Age Past Service Cost and Accumulated Benefits Obligation Due to Change in Actuarial Assumptions and Plan Amendment.

Under current accounting treatment, pension expense will include a provision for amortization of the change in entry age past service cost beginning in year 2. Under the accounting alternative which defines expense as the net change in obligation, the full change in the accumulated benefits obligation due to the change in assumptions or plan amendment is included in pension expense in year 2. The third accounting alternative establishes a deferred charge (credit) to offset the portion of the total change in accumulated benefits obligation which is due to the change in assumptions or plan amendment. Total pension expense then includes a positive (negative) provision representing amortization of this deferred charge (credit).

The table on the opposite page compares pension expense in year 2 upon occurrence of each of the events described above under the three accounting treatments

Note that a change in the interest assumption from 7% to 8% results in a negative pension expense when expense is defined as the net change in obligation, excluding amounts funded.

Accounting Treatment	Pension Expense In Year 2						
	No Gain or Loss, Change in Assumptions or Plan Amendment	Actuarial Loss Equal to 5% of Plan Assets	%*	Increase in Interest Assumption from 7% to 8%	%*	Amend Plan to Increase Benefit Formula	%*
Current treatment-expense amount funded (entry age cost method).	$1,900	$2,000	5%	$1,560	(18%)	$2,130	12%
Expense defined as net change in pension obligation, all changes in obligation charged immediately to income.**	$1,310	$2,400	83%	($1,090)	(183%)	$2,390	82%
Expense defined as net change in pension obligation, except certain obligation changes offset by deferred charges (credits) and amortized.**	$1,360	$1,480	9%	$1,060	(22%)	$1,560	15%

*Percentage increase (decrease) in expense relative to expense if no gain or loss, change in assumptions or plan amendment occurs.

**Pension obligation measured by accumulated benefits.

Comparison of Final Pay Plan Expense Under Alternative Accounting Treatments Upon Occurrence of Actuarial Loss, Change in Assumptions and Plan Amendment. (Amounts in 000's.)

NOTES

1. In a strictly technical sense, the past service cost under the aggregate method is equal to the plan assets. Therefore, under this method the unfunded pension obligation would always be zero. Similarly, for a frozen initial liability method the past service cost can be considered to be equal to the plan assets plus the unfunded portion of the frozen liability (if any).

2. The declining pattern of expense during the first 30 years results from the addition of the constant past service amortization provision to a normal cost which is increasing with compensation. As a result, the total expense of normal cost plus the amortization amount will decline as a percentage of compensation.

3. Most actuaries would prefer the entry age-constant amount cost method over the entry age constant percent of salary cost method in conjunction with a unit benefit plan, since the benefit formula for this type of plan is unrelated to salary. However, since the entry-age constant percent of salary cost method is commonly applied to final pay and career average plans, it is used with the unit benefit plan in this and the next section in order to make a consistent comparison between all three plan types.

4. A decision by an employer to amend his plan may depend on such things as the employer's philosophy with regard to pension benefits, the rate of inflation, competitors' practices and union pressures. The actuary would face a difficult task in selecting an appropriate assumption in the face of these variables. Anticipating future plan amendments indicates a commitment by the plan sponsor which does not exist, and could produce unwarranted expectations for employees. For *funding* purposes, IRS regulations prohibit the anticipation of future amendments in determining minimum required and maximum deductible contribution levels.

5. The PBGC establishes the assumptions to be used in measuring the termination liability of terminating plans based on the current annuity rates of insurers. The PBGC periodically revises its assumptions to reflect changing insurance company rates.

6. These three methods are intended to illustrate the range of alternative accounting treatments discussed in Chapter Five. Other methods are also possible (e.g., offset the initial unfunded obligation by a deferred charge, but charge future obligation increases immediately to income, regardless of the source).

7. This assumes that the pension obligation is measured at the beginning of the company fiscal year. This would be the typical situation for many plans, but the obligation might just as well be measured during or at the end of the fiscal year. When the calculations are made at the beginning, or during the company fiscal year, the change in obligation and assets for the year must be estimated in determining pension expense. This also means that actuarial gains or losses will not be recognized in expense in the year in which they occur, but in the following year.

8. The loss of $1,014,000 results in an increase in expense of $1,090,000. The increase in expense is greater than the loss alone, the difference representing interest which is lost due to the decline in value of the plan's assets.

APPENDIX A

APPENDIX A

DESCRIPTION OF THE MODEL USED IN THE
QUANTITATIVE ANALYSES OF CHAPTER SEVEN

The analysis of alternative methods of measuring pension obligation and expense in Chapter Seven is based on a model pension program. This model consists of the following elements:

- Three model pension plans;

- Three model plan populations projected over a 50-year period composed of active, retired and terminated vested plan members;

- A model set of actuarial assumptions used in the valuation of pension obligation and expense for the model plan.

In addition to the above elements, the analysis of alternative accounting treatments for recording or disclosing pension obligation and expense uses model financial statements for a hypothetical plan sponsor. The following describes in detail the elements of the model.

Model Pension Plans

For the majority of the analysis in Chapter Seven, the model is based on a final pay pension plan. However, in order to study the impact of differing plan provisions on obligation and expense, the model also considers a career average plan and a unit benefit plan (fixed benefit amount for each year of service). Each plan is assumed to be established in year 1 of a 50-year projection period, with years of service worked prior to establishment of the plan credited for both benefits and eligibility for vesting.

Table 1 compares the provisions of the three plans. The benefit formulas of the plans are structured so that a member's accrued benefit at any point in time will be the same under all three plans. To accomplish this requires annual amendments to the career average and unit benefit plans. In this way, the three plans are equivalent in that each provides the same benefit to a retiring or terminating member and the same accrued benefit to an active member, despite the fact that the benefit formulas are very different. Table 2 illustrates this for a single plan member by showing the build-up of the accrued benefit under each plan from age 25 to normal retirement age.

TABLE 1

PROVISIONS OF MODEL PENSION PLANS

	Final Pay Plan	Career Average Plan	Unit Benefit Plan
Eligibility	Age 25.	Age 25.	Age 25.
Vesting	100% after 10 years of service.	100% after 10 years of service.	100% after 10 years of service.
Benefit Formula	1% × (final salary) × years of service.	1% of salary during each year of service; past service benefit at plan inception equal to 1% of salary in previous year times past service.	(Unit benefit) × years of service; unit benefit amount equal to 1% of salary at date plan is established or date of hire, if later.
Annual Amendments	None.	At beginning of each year, total benefit accrued to date is updated to 1% × salary in previous year × service to date.	Unit benefit amount increased by 6% each year.
Normal Retirement	Age 65.	Age 65.	Age 65.
Early Retirement, Disability and Death Benefits	None.	None.	None.

TABLE 2

ACCRUED BENEFITS UNDER THREE MODEL PLANS

Year	Age	Salary	Final Pay Plan Increase in Accrued Benefit Due to Formula	Due to Amendment	Total Accrued Benefit	Career Average Plan Increase in Accrued Benefit Due to Formula	Due to Amendment	Total Accrued Benefit	Unit Benefit Plan Increase in Accrued Benefit Due to Formula	Due to Amendment	Total Accrued Benefit
1	25	15,000.	150.	0.	150.	150.	0.	150.	150.	0.	150.
2	26	15,900.	168.	0.	318.	159.	9.	318.	150.	18.	318.
3	27	16,854.	188.	0.	506.	169.	19.	506.	159.	29.	506.
4	28	17,865.	209.	0.	715.	179.	30.	715.	169.	40.	715.
5	29	18,937.	232.	0.	947.	189.	43.	947.	179.	54.	947.
6	30	20,073.	258.	0.	1,204.	201.	57.	1,204.	189.	68.	1,204.
7	31	21,278.	285.	0.	1,489.	213.	72.	1,489.	201.	84.	1,489.
8	32	22,554.	315.	0.	1,804.	226.	89.	1,804.	213.	102.	1,804.
9	33	23,908.	347.	0.	2,152.	239.	108.	2,152.	226.	122.	2,152.
10	34	25,342.	383.	0.	2,534.	253.	129.	2,534.	239.	143.	2,534.
11	35	26,863.	421.	0.	2,955.	269.	152.	2,955.	253.	167.	2,955.
12	36	28,474.	462.	0.	3,417.	285.	177.	3,417.	269.	193.	3,417.
13	37	30,183.	507.	0.	3,924.	302.	205.	3,924.	285.	222.	3,924.
14	38	31,994.	555.	0.	4,479.	320.	235.	4,479.	302.	254.	4,479.
15	39	33,914.	608.	0.	5,087.	339.	269.	5,087.	320.	288.	5,087.
16	40	35,948.	665.	0.	5,752.	359.	305.	5,752.	339.	326.	5,752.
17	41	38,105.	726.	0.	6,478.	381.	345.	6,478.	359.	367.	6,478.
18	42	40,392.	793.	0.	7,270.	404.	389.	7,270.	381.	412.	7,270.
19	43	42,815.	864.	0.	8,135.	428.	436.	8,135.	404.	460.	8,135.
20	44	45,384.	942.	0.	9,077.	454.	488.	9,077.	428.	514.	9,077.

TABLE 2 (cont.)

ACCRUED BENEFITS UNDER THREE MODEL PLANS

Year	Age	Salary	Final Pay Plan — Increase in Accrued Benefit Due to Formula	Due to Amendment	Total Accrued Benefit	Career Average Plan — Increase in Accrued Benefit Due to Formula	Due to Amendment	Total Accrued Benefit	Unit Benefit Plan — Increase in Accrued Benefit Due to Formula	Due to Amendment	Total Accrued Benefit
21	45	48,107.	1,026.	0.	10,102.	481.	545.	10,102.	454.	572.	10,102.
22	46	50,993.	1,116.	0.	11,219.	510.	606.	11,219.	481.	635.	11,219.
23	47	54,053.	1,214.	0.	12,432.	541.	673.	12,432.	510.	704.	12,432.
24	48	57,296.	1,319.	0.	13,751.	573.	746.	13,751.	541.	778.	13,751.
25	49	60,734.	1,432.	0.	15,183.	607.	825.	15,183.	573.	859.	15,183.
26	50	64,378.	1,555.	0.	16,738.	644.	911.	16,738.	607.	947.	16,738.
27	51	68,241.	1,687.	0.	18,425.	682.	1,004.	18,425.	644.	1,043.	18,425.
28	52	72,335.	1,829.	0.	20,254.	723.	1,106.	20,254.	682.	1,146.	20,254.
29	53	76,675.	1,982.	0.	22,236.	767.	1,215.	22,236.	723.	1,259.	22,236.
30	54	81,276.	2,147.	0.	24,383.	813.	1,334.	24,383.	767.	1,380.	24,383.
31	55	86,152.	2,324.	0.	26,707.	862.	1,463.	26,707.	813.	1,512.	26,707.
32	56	91,321.	2,516.	0.	29,223.	913.	1,602.	29,223.	862.	1,654.	29,223.
33	57	96,801.	2,721.	0.	31,944.	968.	1,753.	31,944.	913.	1,808.	31,944.
34	58	102,609.	2,943.	0.	34,887.	1,026.	1,917.	34,887.	968.	1,975.	34,887.
35	59	108,765.	3,181.	0.	38,068.	1,088.	2,093.	38,068.	1,026.	2,155.	38,068.
36	60	115,291.	3,437.	0.	41,505.	1,153.	2,284.	41,505.	1,088.	2,349.	41,505.
37	61	122,209.	3,712.	0.	45,217.	1,222.	2,490.	45,217.	1,153.	2,559.	45,217.
38	62	129,541.	4,008.	0.	49,226.	1,295.	2,713.	49,226.	1,222.	2,786.	49,226.
39	63	137,313.	4,327.	0.	53,552.	1,373.	2,954.	53,552.	1,295.	3,031.	53,552.
40	64	145,552.	4,669.	0.	58,221.	1,456.	3,213.	58,221.	1,373.	3,296.	58,221.

Many pension plans in the U.S. are integrated with Social Security benefits (i.e., the plan benefit formula reflects, directly or indirectly, the Social Security benefit expected to be paid to a retiring employee). The three pension plans in the model are not integrated with Social Security in order to simplify the mechanics of the modeling process and allow more easily for the comparison of three differing benefit formulas which provide equivalent benefits. The observations and relationships drawn from the model will generally be applicable to both integrated and non-integrated plans.

Similarly some plans in the U.S. provide various ancillary benefits such as liberal early retirement benefits or death and disability benefits. Ancillary benefits are excluded from the model in the interest of simplicity; however, the results of the modeling analysis are generally applicable to plans which include these types of benefits.

Model Plan Populations

The model considers three different plan populations covering the 50-year projection period. Tables 3, 4 and 5 show the characteristics of these populations for each year of the projection.

The population in Table 3 maintains a constant active membership of 1,500 active members throughout the 50-year period. The active population is stationary—the distribution of members by age and service remains constant from one year to the next. Initially, there are no inactive members (retired and terminated vested members) in the population. By year 50, the inactive population is also very near to a stationary state. The stationary population projection is used throughout the modeling analysis to study the effect of various factors on obligation and expense without the complicating influence of a changing plan membership.

The two populations in Tables 4 and 5 exhibit rapid growth initially and are identical for years 1–30. Beginning in year 31, the active membership of one population (Table 4) begins to decline in size while the other (Table 5) continues to maintain a constant size. The table below shows the rates of growth (decline) in the active population in each case.

TABLE 3

MODEL PLAN MEMBERSHIP PROJECTION
STATIONARY ACTIVE POPULATION

Year	Actives					Inactives		
	Number	Total Salary	Average Age	Average Service	Average Salary	Retirees	Vested Terminated	Total Payments
1	1,500.	27,248,288.	43.6	9.1	18,161.	0.	0.	0.
2	1,500.	28,597,040.	43.6	9.1	19,060.	31.	26.	150,644.
3	1,500.	30,013,120.	43.6	9.1	20,004.	60.	53.	305,544.
4	1,500.	31,498,992.	43.6	9.1	20,994.	90.	79.	464,652.
5	1,500.	33,058,672.	43.6	9.1	22,034.	118.	105.	627,926.
6	1,500.	34,695,648.	43.6	9.1	23,125.	146.	131.	795,369.
7	1,500.	36,413,616.	43.6	9.1	24,270.	173.	157.	967,016.
8	1,500.	38,216,240.	43.6	9.1	25,471.	199.	182.	1,142,919.
9	1,500.	40,108,576.	43.6	9.1	26,733.	224.	207.	1,323,213.
10	1,500.	42,094,464.	43.6	9.1	28,056.	248.	232.	1,508,113.
11	1,500.	44,178,720.	43.6	9.1	29,445.	272.	256.	1,697,953.
12	1,500.	46,366,320.	43.6	9.1	30,903.	294.	280.	1,893,118.
13	1,500.	48,661,952.	43.6	9.1	32,433.	317.	302.	2,094,054.
14	1,500.	51,071,584.	43.6	9.1	34,039.	338.	324.	2,301,122.
15	1,500.	53,600,192.	43.6	9.1	35,725.	359.	345.	2,514,666.
16	1,500.	56,254,176.	43.6	9.1	37,494.	379.	365.	2,734,974.
17	1,500.	59,039,616.	43.6	9.1	39,350.	399.	383.	2,962,428.
18	1,500.	61,962,896.	43.6	9.1	41,298.	419.	401.	3,197,372.
19	1,500.	65,030,736.	43.6	9.1	43,343.	438.	417.	3,440,213.
20	1,500.	68,250,912.	43.6	9.1	45,489.	457.	432.	3,691,411.
21	1,500.	71,630,464.	43.6	9.1	47,742.	476.	445.	3,951,478.
22	1,500.	75,176,672.	43.6	9.1	50,106.	494.	456.	4,221,039.
23	1,500.	78,899,248.	43.6	9.1	52,587.	513.	467.	4,500,758.
24	1,500.	82,805,808.	43.6	9.1	55,190.	531.	475.	4,791,234.

TABLE 3 (cont.)

MODEL PLAN MEMBERSHIP PROJECTION
STATIONARY ACTIVE POPULATION

25	1,500.	86,905,760.	43.6	9.1	57,923.	549.	482.	5,093,076.
26	1,500.	91,208,624.	43.6	9.1	60,791.	568.	488.	5,406,959.
27	1,500.	95,724,688.	43.6	9.1	63,801.	586.	492.	5,733,574.
28	1,500.	100,464,176.	43.6	9.1	66,960.	604.	495.	6,073,621.
29	1,500.	105,438,688.	43.6	9.1	70,275.	622.	497.	6,427,611.
30	1,500.	110,659,392.	43.6	9.1	73,755.	640.	498.	6,796,108.
31	1,500.	116,138,352.	43.6	9.1	77,407.	657.	498.	7,179,622.
32	1,500.	121,888,336.	43.6	9.1	81,239.	673.	498.	7,578,676.
33	1,500.	127,923,456.	43.6	9.1	85,261.	688.	498.	7,993,787.
34	1,500.	134,257,248.	43.6	9.1	89,483.	702.	498.	8,426,008.
35	1,500.	140,904,256.	43.6	9.1	93,913.	715.	498.	8,876,453.
36	1,500.	147,880,848.	43.6	9.1	98,563.	727.	498.	9,346,211.
37	1,500.	155,202,928.	43.6	9.1	103,443.	738.	498.	9,836,473.
38	1,500.	162,887,040.	43.6	9.1	108,565.	749.	498.	10,348,391.
39	1,500.	170,951,872.	43.6	9.1	113,940.	758.	498.	10,883,276.
40	1,500.	179,416,096.	43.6	9.1	119,581.	766.	498.	11,442,357.
41	1,500.	188,299,168.	43.6	9.1	125,502.	774.	498.	12,026,995.
42	1,500.	197,622,192.	43.6	9.1	131,716.	781.	498.	12,638,601.
43	1,500.	207,406,800.	43.6	9.1	138,237.	787.	498.	13,278,640.
44	1,500.	217,675,648.	43.6	9.1	145,082.	793.	498.	13,948,622.
45	1,500.	228,452,848.	43.6	9.1	152,265.	798.	498.	14,650,206.
46	1,500.	239,763,760.	43.6	9.1	159,803.	802.	498.	15,385,044.
47	1,500.	251,634,912.	43.6	9.1	167,716.	806.	498.	16,154,933.
48	1,500.	264,093,504.	43.6	9.1	176,019.	809.	498.	16,959,232.
49	1,500.	277,163,520.	43.6	9.1	184,731.	811.	498.	17,802,608.
50	1,500.	290,878,464.	43.6	9.1	193,871.	814.	498.	18,687,952.

TABLE 4

MODEL PLAN MEMBERSHIP PROJECTION
DECLINING ACTIVE POPULATION

Year	Actives					Inactives		
	Number	Total Salary	Average Age	Average Service	Average Salary	Retirees	Vested Terminated	Total Payments
1	1,500.	27,248,288.	43.6	9.1	18,161.	0.	0.	0.
2	1,650.	31,198,384.	42.8	8.2	18,904.	31.	26.	150,644.
3	1,815.	35,774,768.	42.1	7.6	19,706.	61.	53.	305,612.
4	1,997.	41,073,312.	41.6	7.0	20,568.	91.	79.	464,945.
5	2,197.	47,205,904.	41.1	6.6	21,490.	120.	105.	628,716.
6	2,307.	51,990,720.	41.1	6.5	22,541.	149.	131.	797,069.
7	2,422.	57,269,408.	41.0	6.4	23,647.	178.	157.	970,156.
8	2,543.	63,090,576.	41.0	6.4	24,810.	206.	182.	1,148,649.
9	2,670.	69,510,608.	41.0	6.3	26,033.	234.	207.	1,333,051.
10	2,804.	76,590,336.	41.0	6.3	27,319.	262.	232.	1,524,014.
11	2,860.	82,144,096.	41.2	6.4	28,725.	290.	256.	1,722,382.
12	2,917.	88,088,576.	41.4	6.6	30,200.	318.	284.	1,928,647.
13	2,975.	94,444,080.	41.5	6.7	31,744.	346.	315.	2,146,647.
14	3,035.	101,239,296.	41.7	6.8	33,360.	375.	351.	2,378,206.
15	3,095.	108,503,680.	41.8	6.9	35,053.	405.	391.	2,625,314.
16	3,126.	115,213,472.	41.9	7.1	36,852.	436.	432.	2,890,113.
17	3,158.	122,317,552.	42.1	7.3	38,737.	467.	475.	3,171,959.
18	3,189.	129,840,144.	42.2	7.4	40,712.	498.	519.	3,472,280.
19	3,221.	137,806,272.	42.4	7.5	42,782.	530.	564.	3,792,628.
20	3,253.	146,243,088.	42.5	7.6	44,952.	563.	611.	4,134,651.
21	3,253.	153,765,712.	42.7	7.8	47,264.	596.	656.	4,500,132.
22	3,253.	161,654,960.	42.8	8.0	49,689.	629.	700.	4,888,194.
23	3,253.	169,918,960.	43.0	8.2	52,230.	662.	743.	5,308,629.

TABLE 4 (cont.)

MODEL PLAN MEMBERSHIP PROJECTION
DECLINING ACTIVE POPULATION

24	3,253.	178,575,248.	43.1	8.3	54,890.	697.	785.	5,764,739.
25	3,253.	187,642,640.	43.2	8.5	57,677.	732.	826.	6,260,179.
26	3,253.	197,139,536.	43.3	8.6	60,597.	769.	864.	6,798,985.
27	3,253.	207,098,000.	43.4	8.7	63,658.	806.	900.	7,376,504.
28	3,253.	217,535,088.	43.5	8.8	66,866.	843.	934.	8,002,074.
29	3,253.	228,473,024.	43.6	8.9	70,228.	882.	966.	8,679,472.
30	3,253.	239,934,352.	43.6	9.0	73,751.	920.	996.	9,412,942.
31	3,221.	249,651,680.	43.8	9.1	77,513.	960.	1,023.	10,207,088.
32	3,189.	259,731,888.	43.9	9.3	81,457.	998.	1,048.	11,051,543.
33	3,157.	270,174,720.	44.0	9.4	85,588.	1,037.	1,071.	11,966,698.
34	3,125.	280,988,416.	44.1	9.5	89,913.	1,076.	1,091.	12,959,240.
35	3,094.	292,184,320.	44.2	9.6	94,440.	1,116.	1,108.	14,036,718.
36	3,032.	301,006,848.	44.4	9.8	99,277.	1,156.	1,122.	15,207,639.
37	2,971.	310,040,320.	44.5	10.0	104,343.	1,196.	1,134.	16,454,804.
38	2,912.	319,279,104.	44.6	10.1	109,646.	1,238.	1,142.	17,798,768.
39	2,854.	328,721,920.	44.7	10.2	115,192.	1,280.	1,147.	19,254,384.
40	2,797.	338,372,096.	44.8	10.3	120,994.	1,324.	1,147.	20,829,856.
41	2,657.	338,647,040.	45.2	10.7	127,465.	1,370.	1,143.	22,536,288.
42	2,524.	338,810,880.	45.6	11.1	134,239.	1,417.	1,135.	24,341,024.
43	2,398.	338,887,680.	45.9	11.5	141,336.	1,460.	1,125.	26,195,264.
44	2,278.	338,878,464.	46.2	11.8	148,771.	1,500.	1,113.	28,092,304.
45	2,164.	338,777,856.	46.5	12.1	156,555.	1,537.	1,102.	30,024,880.
46	1,959.	324,500,992.	47.3	13.0	165,666.	1,569.	1,089.	31,984,080.
47	1,774.	310,836,480.	48.2	13.8	175,252.	1,598.	1,075.	33,972,144.
48	1,606.	297,701,120.	48.9	14.7	185,335.	1,622.	1,060.	35,983,072.
49	1,455.	285,010,944.	49.7	15.5	195,935.	1,642.	1,044.	38,010,736.
50	1,317.	272,686,336.	50.4	16.4	207,074.	1,658.	1,028.	40,048,992.

TABLE 5

MODEL PLAN MEMBERSHIP PROJECTION
GROWING ACTIVE POPULATION

Year	Actives					Inactives		
	Number	Total Salary	Average Age	Average Service	Average Salary	Retirees	Vested Terminated	Total Payments
1	1,500.	27,248,288.	43.6	9.1	18,161.	0.	0.	0.
2	1,650.	31,198,384.	42.8	8.2	18,904.	31.	26.	150,644.
3	1,815.	35,774,768.	42.1	7.6	19,706.	61.	53.	305,612.
4	1,997.	41,073,312.	41.6	7.0	20,568.	91.	79.	464,945.
5	2,197.	47,205,904.	41.1	6.6	21,490.	120.	105.	628,716.
6	2,307.	51,990,720.	41.1	6.5	22,541.	149.	131.	797,069.
7	2,422.	57,269,408.	41.0	6.4	23,647.	178.	157.	970,156.
8	2,543.	63,090,576.	41.0	6.4	24,810.	206.	182.	1,148,649.
9	2,670.	69,510,608.	41.0	6.3	26,033.	234.	207.	1,333,051.
10	2,804.	76,590,336.	41.0	6.3	27,319.	262.	232.	1,524,014.
11	2,860.	82,144,096.	41.2	6.4	28,725.	290.	256.	1,722,382.
12	2,917.	88,088,576.	41.4	6.6	30,200.	318.	284.	1,928,647.
13	2,975.	94,444,080.	41.5	6.7	31,744.	346.	315.	2,146,647.
14	3,035.	101,239,296.	41.7	6.8	33,360.	375.	351.	2,378,206.
15	3,095.	108,503,680.	41.8	6.9	35,053.	405.	391.	2,625,314.
16	3,126.	115,213,472.	41.9	7.1	36,852.	436.	432.	2,890,113.
17	3,158.	122,317,552.	42.1	7.3	38,737.	467.	475.	3,171,959.
18	3,189.	129,840,144.	42.2	7.4	40,712.	498.	519.	3,472,280.
19	3,221.	137,806,272.	42.4	7.5	42,782.	530.	564.	3,792,628.
20	3,253.	146,243,088.	42.5	7.6	44,952.	563.	611.	4,134,651.
21	3,253.	153,765,712.	42.7	7.8	47,264.	596.	656.	4,500,132.
22	3,253.	161,654,960.	42.8	8.0	49,689.	629.	700.	4,888,194.
23	3,253.	169,918,960.	43.0	8.2	52,230.	662.	743.	5,308,629.

TABLE 5 (cont.)

MODEL PLAN MEMBERSHIP PROJECTION
GROWING ACTIVE POPULATION

24	3,253.	178,575,248.	43.1	8.3	54,890.	697.	785.	5,764.739.
25	3,253.	187,642,640.	43.2	8.5	57,677.	732.	826.	6,260,179.
26	3,253.	197,139,536.	43.3	8.6	60,597.	769.	864.	6,798,985.
27	3,253.	207,098,000.	43.4	8.7	63,658.	806.	900.	7,376,504.
28	3,253.	217,535,088.	43.5	8.8	66,866.	843.	934.	8,002,074.
29	3,253.	228,473,024.	43.6	8.9	70,228.	882.	966.	8,679,472.
30	3,253.	239,934,352.	43.6	9.0	73,751.	920.	996.	9,412,942.
31	3,253.	251,942,512.	43.7	9.0	77,442.	960.	1,023.	10,207,088.
32	3,253.	264,541,376	43.7	9.1	81,314.	998.	1,048.	11,051,603.
33	3,253.	277,740,288.	43.8	9.2	85,372.	1,037.	1,071.	11,966,949.
34	3,253.	291,572,224.	43.8	9.2	89,623.	1,076.	1,091.	12,959,898.
35	3,253.	306,063,360.	43.8	9.2	94,078.	1,116.	1,108.	14,038,095.
36	3,253.	321,244,672.	43.8	9.3	98,744.	1,157.	1,122.	15,210,160.
37	3,253.	337,167,872.	43.8	9.3	103,638.	1,198.	1,134.	16,459,520.
38	3,253.	353,854,976.	43.8	9.3	108,768.	1,240.	1,142.	17,807,088.
39	3,253.	371,338,240.	43.8	9.3	114,142.	1,283.	1,147.	19,268,160.
40	3,253.	389,656,064.	43.8	9.3	119,772.	1,329.	1,147.	20,851,392.
41	3,253.	408,837,888.	43.8	9.2	125,668.	1,376.	1,144.	22,568,352.
42	3,253.	428,955,392.	43.7	9.2	131,852.	1,425.	1,137.	24,390,416
43	3,253.	450,071,808.	43.7	9.2	138,343.	1,471.	1,130.	26,270,400.
44	3,253.	472,243,712.	43.7	9.2	145,158.	1,514.	1,122.	28,203,376
45	3,253.	495,515,136.	43.7	9.1	152,311.	1,554.	1,115.	30,184,000.
46	3,253.	519,951,872.	43.7	9.1	159,822.	1,591.	1,108.	32,205,168.
47	3,253.	545,608,192.	43.6	9.1	167,709.	1,625.	1,102.	34,276,832.
48	3,253.	572,545,280.	43.6	9.1	175,989.	1,655.	1,095.	36,396,528.
49	3,253.	600,832,512.	43.6	9.1	184,684.	1,683.	1,090.	38,562,080.
50	3,253.	630,528,512.	43.6	9.0	193,812.	1,707.	1,085.	40,771,280.

| | Population Growth Rates | | |
Year	Table 3	Table 4	Table 5
2–5	0%	10%	10%
6–10	0%	5%	5%
11–15	0%	2%	2%
16–20	0%	1%	1%
21–30	0%	0%	0%
31–35	0%	(1%)	0%
36–40	0%	(2%)	0%
41–45	0%	(5%)	0%
46–50	0%	no new entrants	0%

Rate of Growth of Active Membership for Model Plan Populations.

As the active population in Table 4 begins to decline, the average age and service of the active membership continually increase. For the active population in Table 5, the average age and service begin to level out and show little fluctuation as the membership remains constant in size from year 20. The population projections shown in Tables 4 and 5 are used in the modeling analysis to study the impact on obligation and expense of a population which shows growth followed by rapid decline (Table 4) and a population which exhibits growth and stability (Table 5).

Much of the analysis in Chapter Seven is concerned with demonstrating the long-term pattern of pension obligation and expense under the influence of different factors. In this analysis, the population projections are considered throughout the entire 50-year period.

At other times, the analysis is limited to considering pension obligation and expense measured at a single point in time when the plan population is immature, mature or overmature. An *immature* population will mean a population with a greater distribution of young, low-service members relative to older, long-service members and with ,few retired members relative to the number of active members. An *overmature* population will mean a population shifted toward older, long-service members, with few new members entering each year and with a large number of retirees relative to active members. A *mature* population will mean a population which has maintained a stable size or rate of growth over a number of years and consequently has attained a stable distribution of members by age and service.

In this type of analysis, the populations in years 10 and 50 of Table 4 represent immature and overmature populations, respectively. The population in year 50 of Table 3 represents a mature population.

The model populations were obtained by defining an initial plan membership in year 1, and then defining a set of parameters which determine the experience of this initial group in subsequent years. The initial membership consists of 1,500 active employees ranging in age from 25 to 64 with years of service from 0 (new hires) to 39 years. Average annual salaries for the group range from $15,000 for the youngest employees to $22,111 for those age 64. The model assumes that all plans are established at the beginning of year 1, hence there are no retired or terminated vested members until year 2.

Table 6 defines the additional parameters which determine the experience of the model plan memberships throughout the projection period. Sufficient new entrants enter the population each year so that, combined with surviving active employees from the previous year, the total active membership attains the size defined by the population growth assumptions.

Actuarial Assumptions for the Model

Table 7 shows the actuarial assumptions used in the model in measuring pension obligation and expense for the model plans and plan populations. These assumptions are used throughout the 50-year projection period.

TABLE 6

PARAMETERS DEFINING EXPERIENCE OF
MODEL PLAN POPULATION

Pre- and Post-Retirement Mortality
    Members experience mortality as defined by the 1971 Group Annuity Mortality Table.

Retirement Age
    All retirements occur at age 65.

Turnover
    Active members experience age-related rates of turnover. Illustrative rates are shown below:

Age	Probability of Withdrawal
25	11.6%
35	10.6
45	7.5
55	1.7

New Entrants
    New members each year are distributed by age as follows:

Entry Age	% of Total New Entrants
25–29	7.6%
30–34	5.0
35–39	2.3
40–44	2.0
45–54	1.0
55–59	0.4
60–64	0.2

The average age of new entrants is 34.

Salary Increases
    Salary increases for active members total 6% per year. Entry level salaries increase at 5% per year.

TABLE 7

ACTUARIAL ASSUMPTIONS USED IN THE MODEL

Pre- and Post-Retirement Mortality	The 1971 Group Annuity Mortality Table (Male).

Turnover — Age-related rates of turnover assumed. Illustrative rates are shown below:

Age	Probability of Withdrawal
25	11.6%
35	10.6%
45	7.5%
55	1.7%

Retirement Age — All retirements assumed to occur at age 65.

Salary Increases — Total of 6% per year consisting of 1% merit, 1% productivity and 4% inflation.

Investment Returns — Total of 7% per year consisting of 3% real return and 4% inflation.

PBGC Assumptions — The PBGC assumptions in effect for plans terminating between December 1, 1979 and February 27, 1980 were used in measuring PBGC obligations. These assumptions included the following interest assumptions:

	Interest Rates
Immediate Annuities	8.50%
Deferred Annuities	
First 7 years	7.75%
Next 8 years	6.50%
All later years	4.00%

The actuarial assumptions with regard to mortality, turnover, age at retirement and salary increases shown in Table 7 are the same as the corresponding parameters in Table 6 which define the experience of the model plan populations. In other words, the actual experience of the model populations is exactly the same as the expected experience predicted by the actuarial assumptions. As a result, no actuarial gains or losses occur in the model throughout the projection period.

Model Employer Financial Statements

Tables 8–11 in the modeling analyses of Chapter Seven illustrate the impact of alternative methods of accounting for pension costs on the financial statements of a typical employer. The hypothetical financial statements used in these illustrations are based on the recent financial statements of several large manufacturing companies. The following describes the assumptions underlying the sample statements.

- Pension obligation and expense—Data relating to the hypothetical company's pension plan is taken from the modeling analysis of the final pay pension plan for years 47–50 of the stationary population projection (Appendix A, Table 3). This basic data is divided by a factor of 10 in order to make it realistic in today's dollars. Pension obligation and expense are then determined under the accounting alternatives described in Chapter Seven.

- Total expense—Total expense in year 1 is assumed to be 200 times pension expense (under current accounting rules). Total expense in years 2 and 3 is assumed to be approximately 93% of annual revenue. Total expense includes income taxes.

- Revenue—Annual revenue in year 1 of the model financials is 107% of the previously calculated total expense. Revenue increases 15% in year 2 and 18% in year 3.

- Assets—Total assets in year 1 are set at 10 times net income for the year (under current accounting treatment). Assets increase 18% during year 2 and 20% during year 3. Current assets are assumed to be 65% of total assets each year.

- Liabilities and stockholders' equity—Stockholders' equity in year 1 is approximately 60% of total liabilities and equity. In subsequent years, equity is increased by income for the year. Current liabilities are assumed to be 22% of total liabilities and equity.

APPENDIX B

APPENDIX B

MODELING RESULTS FOR MODEL FINAL PAY PLAN

Much of the analysis of pension obligation and expense in Chapter Seven uses the model final pay pension plan and the three plan population projections described in Appendix A.

The following Tables 1 – 3 show the results of the modeling for the final pay plan under the obligation measures and actuarial cost methods considered in Chapter Seven. The data is based on the three model population projections and the model assumptions described in Appendix A. For the cost methods, both the past service cost (pension obligation) and normal cost are shown.

TABLE 1

MODELING RESULTS FOR FINAL PAY PLAN
AND STATIONARY ACTIVE POPULATION PROJECTION
(Amounts in 000's)

Year	No. Actives	Total Salaries	Pension Obligation				Accrued Benefit Cost Method		Accrued Benefit – Salary Prorate Cost Method		Accrued Benefit – Service Prorate Cost Method		Entry Age – Constant Percent of Salary Cost Method		Entry Age – Constant Amount Cost Method		Aggregate Cost Method	
			PBGC Guaranteed Benefits	Vested Benefits	Accumulated Benefits	Benefits At Risk	Past Service Cost	Normal Cost	Past Service Cost	Normal Cost	Past Service Cost	Normal Cost	Past Service Cost	Normal Cost	Past Service Cost	Normal Cost	Past Service Cost	Normal Cost
1	1,500	$27,250	$ 0	$ 8,180	$ 9,140	$ 9,310	$ 9,140	$1,180	$10,770	$1,160	$14,400	$1,090	$18,460	$1,000	$21,050	$ 950	—	$2,970
2	1,500	28,600	1,770	10,050	11,060	11,240	11,060	1,240	12,770	1,220	16,580	1,140	20,837	1,050	23,560	1,000	—	2,930
3	1,500	30,010	4,220	11,960	13,020	13,210	13,020	1,300	14,820	1,280	18,820	1,200	23,290	1,100	26,150	1,050	—	2,900
4	1,500	31,500	7,380	13,920	15,030	15,230	15,030	1,370	16,920	1,340	21,110	1,260	25,800	1,160	28,800	1,100	—	2,870
5	1,500	33,060	11,280	15,920	17,080	17,290	17,080	1,440	19,070	1,410	23,470	1,320	28,390	1,210	31,540	1,150	—	2,850
10	1,500	42,090	23,760	26,690	28,180	28,440	28,180	1,830	30,700	1,790	36,310	1,680	42,570	1,540	46,580	1,470	—	2,860
20	1,500	68,250	47,980	53,750	56,150	56,580	56,150	2,970	60,250	2,910	69,330	2,720	79,490	2,500	86,000	2,380	—	3,400
30	1,500	110,660	83,030	92,970	96,870	97,560	96,870	4,810	103,510	4,710	118,240	4,410	134,710	4,060	145,260	3,860	—	4,780
40	1,500	179,420	136,790	153,120	159,440	160,560	159,440	7,790	170,200	7,640	194,100	7,150	220,800	6,580	237,900	6,250	—	7,310
50	1,500	290,880	222,340	248,870	259,130	260,940	259,130	2,640	276,570	12,380	315,310	11,590	358,600	10,670	386,340	10,140	—	11,600

219

TABLE 2

MODELING RESULTS FOR FINAL PAY PLAN AND GROWING ACTIVE POPULATION
(Amounts in 000's)

Year	No. Actives	Total Salaries	PBGC Guaranteed Benefits	Vested Benefits	Accu-mulated Benefits	Benefits At Risk	Accrued Benefit Cost Method Past Service Cost	Normal Cost	Accrued Benefit – Salary Prorate Cost Method Past Service Cost	Normal Cost	Accrued Benefit – Service Prorate Cost Method Past Service Cost	Normal Cost	Entry Age – Constant Percent of Salary Cost Method Past Service Cost	Normal Cost	Entry Age – Constant Amount Cost Method Past Service Cost	Normal Cost
1	1,500	$27,250	$ 0	$ 8,180	$ 9,140	$ 9,310	$ 9,140	$1,180	$10,770	$1,160	$14,400	$1,090	$18,460	$1,000	$21,050	$ 950
2	1,650	31,200	1,770	10,050	11,060	11,240	11,060	1,260	12,770	1,250	16,580	1,190	20,840	1,140	23,560	1,140
3	1,815	35,770	4,220	11,960	13,020	13,240	13,020	1,350	14,850	1,340	18,870	1,310	23,390	1,310	26,300	1,350
4	1,997	41,070	7,380	13,920	15,030	15,330	15,030	1,450	17,020	1,460	21,290	1,450	26,140	1,510	29,290	1,590
5	2,197	47,210	11,280	15,930	17,250	17,520	17,250	1,560	19,300	1,590	23,860	1,610	29,120	1,730	32,580	1,870
10	2,804	76,590	23,880	26,820	29,860	30,480	29,860	2,320	32,960	2,420	39,820	2,570	48,330	2,840	54,190	3,060
20	3,253	146,240	61,320	68,430	74,040	75,030	74,040	5,150	81,460	5,270	97,830	5,430	117,920	5,460	131,530	5,440
30	3,253	239,930	140,640	157,870	166,160	167,630	166,160	10,070	180,750	9,980	213,150	9,570	249,790	8,860	273,380	8,370
40	3,253	389,660	283,810	318,700	332,180	334,570	332,180	17,450	356,070	17,000	409,140	15,680	467,640	14,250	504,790	13,450
50	3,253	630,530	489,160	547,400	569,730	573,680	569,730	27,430	607,370	26,860	690,910	25,090	784,250	23,120	844,070	22,000

TABLE 3

MODELING RESULTS FOR FINAL PAY PLAN AND DECLINING ACTIVE POPULATION
(Amounts in 000's)

Year	No. Actives	Total Salaries	Pension Obligation PBGC Guaranteed Benefits	Vested Benefits	Accumulated Benefits	Benefits At Risk	Accrued Benefit Cost Method Past Service Cost	Normal Cost	Accrued Benefit – Salary Prorate Cost Method Past Service Cost	Normal Cost	Accrued Benefit – Service Prorate Cost Method Past Service Cost	Normal Cost	Entry Age – Constant Percent of Salary Cost Method Past Service Cost	Normal Cost	Entry Age – Constant Amount Cost Method Past Service Cost	Normal Cost
1	1,500	$27,250	$ 0	$ 8,180	$ 9,140	$ 9,310	$ 9,140	$1,180	$10,770	$1,160	$14,400	$1,090	$18,460	$1,000	$21,050	$ 950
2	1,650	31,200	1,770	10,050	11,060	11,240	11,060	1,260	12,770	1,250	16,580	1,190	20,840	1,140	23,560	1,140
3	1,815	35,770	4,220	11,960	13,020	13,240	13,020	1,350	14,850	1,340	18,870	1,310	23,390	1,310	26,300	1,350
4	1,997	41,070	7,380	13,920	15,030	15,330	15,030	1,450	17,020	1,460	21,290	1,450	26,140	1,510	29,290	1,590
5	2,197	47,210	11,280	15,930	17,250	17,520	17,250	1,560	19,300	1,590	23,860	1,610	29,120	1,730	32,580	1,870
10	2,804	76,590	23,880	26,820	29,860	30,480	29,860	2,320	32,960	2,420	39,820	2,570	48,330	2,840	54,190	3,060
20	3,253	146,240	61,320	68,430	74,040	75,030	74,040	5,150	81,460	5,270	97,830	5,430	117,920	5,460	131,530	5,440
30	3,253	239,930	140,640	157,870	166,160	167,630	166,160	10,070	180,750	9,980	213,150	9,570	249,790	8,860	273,380	8,370
40	2,797	338,370	283,650	318,520	329,960	331,890	329,960	16,760	353,110	16,110	404,540	14,400	460,080	12,330	494,790	11,050
50	1,317	272,690	469,560	525,870	532,590	533,380	532,590	20,800	561,500	19,040	625,940	14,870	689,430	9,670	726,220	6,240

EIGHT

OBSERVATIONS OF COOPERS & LYBRAND'S RESEARCH TEAM

As a result of the study, the Coopers & Lybrand research team developed certain observations and opinions on accounting for pension costs and other post-retirement benefits. These observations and opinions are discussed in this chapter and should be construed as solely the views of the Coopers & Lybrand research team and not those of the Financial Executives Research Foundation Project Advisory Committee or anyone else connected with the study.

EMPLOYER ACCOUNTING FOR PENSION COSTS

Our research indicates that there is a definite need for improved accounting principles for pension costs. Current accounting practice (APB Opinion No. 8 and FASB Statement No. 36) requires a defined benefit plan sponsor to disclose information that includes:

- Pension expense for the period,
- The actuarial present value of accumulated benefits, broken down by vested and non-vested benefits, and
- The market value of plan assets.

There is great concern that this information does not meaningfully portray the financial effect of an employer's pension plan responsibilities. We share this concern and believe that in most cases this information does not permit appropriate analysis of pension expense and obligation. It should be noted that there is generally no direct relationship between annual pension expense and the actuarial present value of accumulated plan benefits. Moreover, since the accumulation of plan assets depends on the sponsor's funding policy and actuarial cost method, there is no direct relationship between the present value of accumulated plan benefits and the market value of plan assets available for those benefits. As a result, an analysis of pension expense, obligation, and plan assets has little meaning without additional information such as:

- The actuarial cost method and assumptions used to determine expense and fund the plan,

- The accrued liability under that cost method,

- The present value of accumulated benefits incorporating a salary assumption,

- Significant changes in the market value of plan assets, and

- Plan amendments.

During the course of the study, we found that a large segment of the financial community did not fully understand these implications.

Based on our research, there seemed to be general agreement that whether an obligation for pension benefits is recorded as an accounting liability or disclosed in a footnote, adequate information should be provided so users of financial statements can understand these amounts. However, the objective of providing meaningful data should be balanced against the concern that if too much information is provided on pension costs, confusion may result. Furthermore, we believe that the relative importance of pension cost information should be balanced against the need to provide other significant financial statement data.

Our survey results indicate that a majority of respondents (61%) believe that a plan sponsor's obligation for pension benefits should not be recorded as a liability. However, there was a wide divergence of opinion between actuaries and independent public accountants.

Of the actuaries surveyed, 69% were opposed to recording a liability; on the other hand, 73% of the surveyed accountants favored recording a liability. It is our view that this important issue should be an integral part of the FASB's conceptual examination of the objectives of financial statements.

Our survey results also indicated a strong reaction against requiring plan sponsors to determine expense using the same actuarial cost method. Furthermore, there was strong opposition to mandating specific values for the actuarial assumptions. Numerous respondents indicated that the current guidelines for determining expense in APB Opinion No. 8 are appropriate.

To develop better accounting principles for pension costs, we recommend that the FASB work closely with the financial community. It is essential that the FASB consider the views of plan sponsors, users of financial statements, actuaries, and accountants when analyzing the complex issues. In particular, we emphasize the FASB's need to work closely with the actuarial profession because the actuarial process is central to the major issues on accounting for pension costs.

Throughout the project we were sensitive to problems involving terminology. A number of interview respondents either criticized or did not fully understand the meaning of certain terms such as prior service costs. By working closely with the actuarial profession and others, commonly understood terminology can be developed and the issues effectively resolved.

OTHER POST-RETIREMENT BENEFITS

We recommend that additional research be conducted to analyze the characteristics and extent of post-retirement health and death benefits currently being provided. Although many companies are providing these benefits to retirees, there is relatively little information available concerning the benefits or their cost.

To better understand the characteristics and magnitude of post-retirement health and death benefits, we believe that analyses and projections are needed that take into account the relevant factors—benefits provided, cost methods to estimate expense, assumptions, characteristics of the covered group of employees, and the financing arrangements for the benefits. There are no guidelines concerning appropriate cost methods and assumptions. We recommend that the methodology for allocating costs be developed and the aforementioned analyses and projections be completed before any new accounting principles are proposed for these benefits. Again, we urge that the FASB work closely with the financial community, particularly the actuarial profession.